MY JOB Gen Z

To Shrestha;

May your work inspire
and bless you, this year as
a graduate fellow) and in all
the years to follow !

— Suzanne Skees
California 2021

MY JOB Gen Z

Finding Your Place in a Fast-Changing World

MY JOB, Volume 3

Suzanne Skees
Sanam Yusuf

Skees Family Foundation

MY JOB Gen Z: Finding Your Place in a Fast-Changing World

Skees Family Foundation

ISBN (paperback): 9781662904264
eISBN: 9781662904271

For Alexis, Sarah, Tessa, Tori, Michael, Daniel, Matthew, Morgan, Michaela, and all the Gen Zers in my family: I love and respect you. Thank you for giving me hope for the future of our world.

— *Suzanne*

To my mother Paru and my father Zia, for always telling me that my age didn't define my place in the world, and for reminding me that I can do anything I dream.

— *Sanam*

CONTENTS

Acknowledgments   XV

Preface: We ARE Gen Z   1

Prologue: The Rising Power of Gen Z   7

Chapter 1: How Gen Z Works   17

    How We Define Generation Z   17

    What People Call Generation Z   18

    Fast, Savvy and No B.S.   18

    What the Statistics Show   19

    Infographics Show Ways Gen Z Is Different   20

    The Surprising Qualities of Gen Z   24

    The One Thing Gen Zers Want Most at Work   26

    Not Their Parents' or Grandparents' Work-World   26

        Kyle

        Michael

        Siddhant

        Mia

        Marie

        Daniel

Constant Adaptation to New Technology   29
    Parker
    Sydney
    Chase
    Shaked

Working from the Ground Up Toward the Dream Goal   31
    Ariel
    Melissa
    Will
    Joanna
    Becka

Instinct for Entrepreneurism   34
    Kian
    Jazmine

Drive Toward Impact Over Money   35
    Sam
    Sydney
    Ella
    Kylene

Facing Age Discrimination   37
    Donna

The Insecurity of the Gig Economy   38
    Chloe

Chapter 2: "Ordinary" Gen Zers Building Extraordinary Careers   39

    Catherine, 18, University Student   40
    Danielle, 26, TSA Officer for the Department of
    Homeland Security   42
    Josiah, 19, Gap Year   46
    Kamrie, 24, Freelance Real Estate Photographer and Stager 48
    Kelly, 17, Office Admin for Hulu   50
    Kristen, 24, International Facility Manager   52

Kristina, 18, Restaurant Waitress and Hostess 54

Lana, 19, Online Tutor 56

Matthew, 22, Electrical Engineering Intern 58

Michael L., 21, Airframe Mechanic for the U.S. Marine Corps 60

Michael T., 19, Legislative Aide to State Senator 62

Morgan, 22, Civil Engineering Intern 64

Pilar, 24, Dietetic Technician at an Eating Disorder Clinic 66

Rachel, 23, Hospital Employee Orientation Trainer 68

Renn, 23, Nursing Home Activities Director 70

Siddhant, 21, Hospital Intern 72

Talia, 18, Lifeguard 74

Tessa, 22, Grocery Store Clerk 76

Theodore, 24, Pornographic Webcam Model 78

Chapter 3: Dream Jobs 81

Who's in This Chapter? 81

How Did They Get There? 81

Apparel and Fashion 84

Brennan Agranoff, 13, HoopSwagg/PetParty 84

Isabella Rose Taylor, 8, Isabella Rose Taylor 86

Moziah Bridges, 9, Mo's Bows 88

Beauty and Body Products 90

Daniel Schlessinger, 18, FixMySkin 90

Isabella Dymalovski, 14, Luv Ur Skin 92

Kiowa Kavovit, 7, Boo Boo Goo 94

Entertainment 96

David Dobrik, 17, David Dobrik's Vlogs 96

Gloson Teh, 12, Poet/Musician/App Developer 98

Jeffrey Owen Hanson, 12, Painter 100

Jojo Siwa, 11, Dancer, Singer, Actor 102

Liza Koshy, 17, Comedian 104

Environment 106

Greta Thunberg, 16, Environmental Activist/
Fridays for Future 106
Hannah Herbst, 17, Inventor 108
Jasilyn Charger, 18, Our Climate Voices 110
Miranda Wang and Jeanny Yao, 22 and 21, BioCellection 112

Finance 114

Aaron Easaw, 18, Maatar Makers 114
Erik Finman, 14, Bitcoin Investor 116
Vitalik Buterin, 19, "Initial Coin Offerings" for
Bitcoin/Ethereum 118

Food and Nutrition 120

Abby Kircher, 15, Abby's Better 120
Cory Nieves, 6, Mr. Cory's Cookies 122
Haile Thomas, 12, Healthy Active Positive
Purposeful Youth (HAPPY) 124
Mikaila Ulmer, 15, Me and the Bees Lemonade 126

Gaming and Sports 128

Kylian Mbappe, 16, Fútbol/Soccer 128
Soleil "EwOk" Wheeler, 13, Fortnite Player 130
Sumail Hassan Syed, 8, Esports Champion 132

Impact 134

Alex Wind, Cameron Kasky, Jaclyn Corin, David
Hogg, and Emma González, 17 to 19, #NeverAgain/
Gun Control, Genocide, and Human Rights Advocates 134
Desmond Napoles, 12, Desmond Is Amazing/"Drag
Kid" and LGBTQIA Advocate 136
Isra Hirsi, 16, U.S. Youth Climate Strike/Activist 138
Kelvin Doe, 11, Electrical Engineer 140
Malala Yousafzai, 15, Education Activist 142
Mihir Garimella, 17, Inventor of Flybrix Tiny Drone 144
Shamma bint Suhail Faris Mazrui, 22, Youth Advocacy 146

Internet 148

Adam Hildreth, 14, Dubit Limited/Crisp Thinking 148

Adam Horwitz, 15, Dirty Laundry/Mobile Monopoly   150
Carl Ocab, 13, Internet Marketing Services/Rich Kid Media 152
Christian Owens, 14, Mac Bundle Box/Branchr Advertising 154
John Xie, 13, Cirtex/Taskade   156
Juliette Brindak, 16, MissOandFriends   158
Nick D'Aloisio, 17, Summly/Sphere Knowledge   160
Noa Mintz, 12, Nannies by Noa   162
Stephen Ou, 25, OhBoard and Other Ventures   164

Marketing   **166**
Farrhad Acidwalla, 16, Rockstah Media   166
Jesse Kay, 17, 20 Under 20s Podcast   168

Retail   **170**
Asia Newson, 5, Super Business Girl/Pretty Brown Girl 170
Ben Pasternak, 17, Several Startups, Currently Nuggs   172
Benjamin "Kickz" Kapelushnik, 16, Sneakerdon.com   174
Maddie Bradshaw, 10, M3 Girl Designs   176
Nic Bianchi, 12, Bianchi Candle Co.   178
Rachel Zietz, 13, Gladiator Lacrosse   180
Sean Belnick, 14, BizChair   182

Social and Racial Justice   **184**
Akil Riley and Xavier Brown, Both 19, Black Lives
Matter Protestor Activists   184
Amika George, 20, Free Periods   186
Brea Baker, 25, Justice League NYC   188
Hadiqa Bashir, 13, Girls United for Human Rights   190
Joshua Wong, 23, Scholarism   192
Nupol Kiazolu, 18, Youth Coalition for Black Lives
Matter of Greater New York/ Vote2000   194
Thandiwe Abdullah, 16, Black Lives Matter Youth
Vanguard, Black Lives Matter in School Program   196
Ziad Ahmed, 21, JUV Consulting   198

Social Media   **200**
EvanTube, 8, EvanTube   200
Evan Spiegel and Bobby Murphy, 21 and 23, Snapchat   202

Kristopher Tate, 20, Zoomr, EVER/IP, connectFree k.k.   204
Loren Gray, 12, Musician   206
Ryan Kaji, 2, Ryan Toys Review/Ryan's World   208

STEM and Technology   210
Jason Li, 15, iReTron   210
Omar Raiyan Azlan, 11, Mathematician/Soccer Player   212
Shubham Banerjee, 12, Braigo Labs   214

Transportation   216
Caleb Nelson, 16, Romeo's Rickshaws   216
George Matus, 18, Teal   218
Ray Land, 17, Fabulous Coach Lines   220

Travel and Real Estate   222
Alex Hodara, 21, Hodara Real Estate Group   222
Bella Tipping, 12, Kidzcationz.com   224

Chapter 4: Achieving YOUR Dream: How-Tos and Further Resources   227

Job-Hunting During the COVID Pandemic   227
Internships: Research the Position You Desire   234
Cover Letter/Email How-Tos   235
Compose a Succinct Resume   239
Use the Right Keywords in Your Resume   242
How To Create a Powerful Profile on LinkedIn   242
How To Use Your Phone To Find a Job   245
How To Capture an Employer's Attention in 6 Seconds   246
How To Organize and Track Your Job Search   246
How To Interview To Get the Job You Want   250
Best Practices After the Interview   259
Tips and Tools   262

Epilogue: Where We Find Hope   291

Sources   295

Endnotes   321

About the Authors   336

Acknowledgments

We honor our families, who supported us through this effort to connect and empower young people:

Maya Chawla, who shared her artistic talent via our book cover design.

Jason Pettus and **Tricia Bohanon** from Gatekeeper Press, who assisted with copyediting and production of our book.

Sarah Helly, for lending advice to and fact-checking the manuscript.

Connie Liu, for her passion that young people can do anything they believe in, and for inspiring Sanam to follow her dreams.

Vincent Oviedo and **Isaac Hinman**, Suzanne's heroes in every way.

We salute the Gen Zers who responded to our survey and shared their values, vision and job stories. Those who shared more than quick-click answers are listed here; find their words woven into the stories of this book. (Note that some respondents chose not to include their surnames.)

Aditi Marshan
Ariela Rosenzweig
Audrey Cho
Catherine Laugharn
Charlie Franklin Love
Chase Hilleary
Chloe Johnson
Daniel Mozes
Danielle Battle
Donna Rowshan
Ella Keinan
Izzy Goldfarb
Izzy Philippe
Jasmin
Jazmine Coburn
Jennifer Dakkak
Joanna L. Grana-Maciel
Josiah Hirsch
Kamrie McKay
Kelly Bignardi
Kian Motamed-Zaman
Kristen
Kristina Stevens
Kyle Toler
Kylene Madrigal
Lana Gesinsky

Marie Cisne
Matthew Maertz
Melissa Brear
Mia McFarland
Michael Lesko
Michael Turner
Mika Kurland Fuchs
Morgan Jackson
Parker Jay-Pachirat
Pilar
Rachel Mayer
Rebecka Yaeger
Roberta Jreisat
Sabrina "Renn" Salkind
Sam Abrahams
Saumya Shinde
Sedona Yates
Shaked
Siddhant Jain
Sydney Cameron
Sydney Shepard
Talia Kurtz
Tessa Skees
Theodore Toler
Victoria Lesko
Will Korsh

We believe that true, inspiring stories of Gen Zers could fill many volumes. However, in this book, our profiled Gen Zers hail from twenty-two countries and thirty-one U.S. states:

Australia
Belgium
Canada
China
Croatia
Egypt
France
India
Israel
Italy
Jordan
Malaysia
Pakistan
Palestine
Philippines
Sierra Leone
Spain
Sweden
United Arab
Emirates

UNITED KINGDOM:
England
Scotland

UNITED STATES:
Alabama
Arizona
California

Colorado
Connecticut
Florida
Georgia
Hawaii
Idaho
Illinois
Indiana
Kansas
Kentucky
Maine
Maryland
Massachusetts
Michigan
Minnesota
Nebraska
New Jersey
New York
Ohio
Oregon
Pennsylvania
South Dakota
Tennessee
Texas
Utah
Washington (State)
Washington, D.C.
Wisconsin

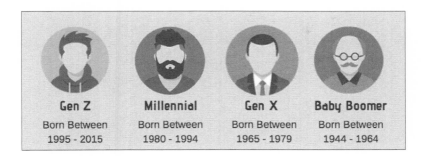

What's a Gen Zer? While sources vary in the dates that define generations, this is the breakdown we use in this book.

See this informative article[1] that reveals shared qualities found within each generation—and the cultural/historical events that shaped us.

Graphic used with permission from kasasa.com.

Preface: We ARE Gen Z
By Sanam Yusuf

"You're Too Young" — I Don't Think So!

So many people tell me, "You're too young to write a book." But I also hear others say, "The future belongs to you; you can do this!" And the truth is that I am young, but the future *is* mine and I *will* do this. My name is Sanam Yusuf and I am a Gen Zer.

The Path That Led Me to This Book

I met the MY JOB book series[2] author Suzanne Skees several years ago. Despite the differences in our ages and life experiences, we just clicked. She became someone I admired and adored. And then, she wrote books!! Books about real people and real lives, genuine stories of incredible people around the world. I loved the idea of creating this community around the world through just having a job.

A few years later, she asked me to collaborate with her on a book. Why me? I don't write books. But she said, "Because this book is about your generation, and I need you for your authentic voice and powerful connections." And thus was born the third book in the MY JOB series: *Gen Z.*

By Gen Z, for Gen Z

You might be asking yourself, why a book about young people? We may not have "real" jobs yet. We might be just scooping ice cream, bussing tables or babysitting. But we have aspirations, hopes, dreams and desires; and this book is about helping those become reality, by:

- Showing what sets us apart from all previous generations—who we are and what we desire from our careers;
- Offering real-life examples of Gen Zers pursuing their dream jobs, revealing common experiences Gen Zers face in the rapidly changing work-world;
- Profiling famous Gen Zers who've had national or global impact at a young age, highlighting the passion and ambition we all have; and,
- Listing best-practice tips on how to discover, obtain and succeed in *your* dream job, so that you can go from dreaming to attaining **right now**.

This book features true accounts from Gen Zers around the world, sharing their own job stories. We asked questions like, *What was your first job? What is your dream job? How will your career differ from your parents'? What's most important to you in a job?* Their job stories range from webcam porn actor to interior designer, partner at an accounting firm, and doctor-in-training.

We Are Completely Different from Previous Generations

How do I know Gen Z is different from any cohort in history? Let me tell you how. We're unique, innovative, and motivated. We're design thinkers and teammates. And we diverge sharply from the conventional way of doing things.

We believe the creation of a successful environment will lead to profitable endeavors in the workplace. Employers should be open to creating new jobs that may be unheard of, and helping people develop their careers in ways that will be useful to both the company but also the skills of their employees.

Most Gen Zers will not stay in the same job their whole life; if we did, we'd be robots. That's why we're looking for managers and companies that will help us be successful both in our current job *and* future endeavors.

Somehow, We Believe in Ourselves and Each Other

We believe strongly in innovation, design thinking, and new ideas. I hear so many people around me say that no idea is a stupid idea. And it's true! The world right now has the power to develop virtually any idea or concept, and when we invest time in every proposal, we open the door to creativity and thinking outside the box. We are Gen Z and somehow, some way, we're optimists.

One of my teachers, Connie Liu, implemented a program at my high school called Project Invent[3], which empowers and supports students to develop and engineer their own products for social good. The project began at a small school in Northern California and has since spread across the United States, with students designing their own products and thus mastering problem-solving skills, learning how to become advocates for their own ideas.

Connie exemplified for me what it meant to believe in Gen Z. She didn't think she had the best ideas that students could work with; instead, she gave us tools and skills that allowed us to bring our ideas to life in the real world. Connie's passion translated into our work, highlighting products made by Gen Z and for social good. It is with this same belief and faith that Connie had in us that Gen Zers will drive change and innovation in the future.

What We Want from our Job and Workspace

We want our work environment to be a place we enjoy going to, a physically attractive space. I've spent 17 of the 19 years of my life so far in school, and I've dreaded it. Waking up early, spending seven hours in one building, coming home to hours of homework.

But what if the places where we went to work weren't boring? Gen Zers, and anyone really, thrive in domains that are comfortable to them. People want to be together for a collective purpose. More and more offices are abandoning the cubicle and adopting large open tables, and there's a reason for this. When you feel you are in a community that supports you and respects you, you want to do the work. The company culture makes you want to be there.

My father, a senior partner and managing director at the Boston Consulting Group[4], recently helped open their new Silicon Valley office based on the principle that "the physical environment you work in drives collaboration, happiness, and overall productivity. An open-plan office," he explains, "with appropriate rooms for team collaboration, is a proven approach in Silicon Valley to drive *breakthrough thinking.*" For him, the spaces we are in and the people we are surrounded with "drive" us to be better workers, better collaborators, and better people. This is a type of place where I wouldn't mind working!

Global Citizens Who Give a Damn

We Gen Zers have a yearning to help the world around us. It's no longer enough just to be passive bystanders while people in our own communities and around the world aren't as fortunate. Taking care of our own is just not good enough for Gen Z. That's why companies that put in real effort, time and money toward their communities and environment attract people my age.

And we love everyone. We want our workplace to be one that provides space and open arms to all kinds of people. A company that focuses on diversity, equity and inclusion is imperative to us. Because if we can't work together in the workplace, how can we work together to change the world?

Disrupted Again, This Time by Pandemic and Recession

Right now, we are facing an unprecedented time. Our jobs are happening from our living rooms and bedrooms; our personal and public lives are slowly blending; and our "normal" way of life has been changed drastically. We could choose to see this as a negative. It's bothersome and disadvantages us because maybe we missed graduation or prom, or our summer plans were cancelled.

Or we can choose to see it as a positive. Nothing like this has happened in your life and likely won't happen again. Use it! Do something creative and take advantage of this time.

I invite you to take part in my generation's journey in the workplace in the pages of this book. ... See what we're made of and what we can do in the world.

Cheers,
Sanam

Prologue: The Rising Power of Gen Z
By Suzanne Skees

The World You Were Born Into—and the Pandemic You Graduated Into

You entered life during the Great Recession, watching your Millennial and Gen X/Y parents lose their jobs, homes and an average 45 percent[5] of net worth; perhaps that's how you turned out so frugal. Now, unlike your predecessors, you earn your own spending money—even as a teenager (77 percent).[6] You exhibit self-reliance and a drive to earn money that surpasses any earlier generation.

Your earliest memory may be the 9-11-2001 terrorist attacks on the New York City World Trade Center towers, the Pentagon, and Flight 93—or, perhaps you're too young to have a conscious memory, but its history is written deep inside you. Front of mind may be the Parkland High School and far too many other mass shootings, as well as the "Me, Too" movement. These pivotal events shaped you during your formative years.

Then, just as you were trying to finish school or get hired, the COVID pandemic struck. It had a massive impact both globally — isolating people who lost their jobs and watched their savings shrink in the inevitable recession — and deeply personally, keeping you away from your friends, your college, your dating life, your independence, and your plans for your life.

You've literally grown up with post-traumatic stress already in your bloodstream. No wonder your top priorities for your career are finding personal stability and creating global impact. You wish for safety and security for yourself and to make the world safe, too.

Now, whether you're navigating unemployment forms, online coursework, or drive-through commencement ceremonies, you've suddenly been propelled into a global reality you might not have believed prior to 2020: the COVID era. You may have moved home from college or retreated deep into your room, hoping the pandemic would quickly pass, only to discover that the virus morphed and invaded not just every geographic area but every aspect of your life.

Nearly one third[7] of Gen Zers aged sixteen and up have lost a job this year; many students cannot find part-time or summer work. Because so many of you worked in high-risk industries such as hospitality and transportation, you've been hit disproportionately by the loss of jobs that may never return. Gen Zers face accompanying depression, isolation, and—I would proffer—powerlessness in the face of what used to seem like your future.

The good news is, you belong to a generation unprecedented in its creative adaptability and problem-solving skills.

Adaptive Coping Skills for a Head-Spinning World

Despite your natural savvy for technology, you still prefer real-life, in-person interactions. You value communication and problem-solving (as contrasted with Millennials' reading and math skills) as the top two assets needed in the workplace.

Often, you turn to YouTube to learn new skills (85 percent viewed at least one teaching video this week). And why not? It's free and often far more relevant than a college course that costs a lifetime of debt.

When seeking employment, you value a fun and flexible work environment over training, promotions, and paid time off.

The work world to which you must adapt changes almost too rapidly for you to keep pace. And you face challenges far beyond your predecessors:

- Artificial intelligence
- Robotics
- Constant online connectivity
- Globalization versus nationalism
- Rising cost of living, looming recession, and unbearable college debt
- Irrelevance of academic study to actual job skills needed
- Climate change and weather crises
- School and public-venue shootings and pervasive lack of safety
- Income and job instability
- Gig economy and the need to work several jobs

- Lack of benefits such as medical insurance and retirement pensions
- Outdated workplaces run on bureaucratic tradition over innovation

Career options have shifted from industry and service to technology and marketing. Now it seems that jobs are all about the *gig economy*—cobbling together enough contracts to pay the bills—and the *hustle*—selling yourself and/or your idea or product.

No Safety Net, from the Office to the Government

An astonishing 12 percent[8] of Gen Zers (as young as 14) have already begun to save for retirement. You hope for, but don't expect, supplemental government assistance. The numbers have transposed when it comes to debt: Millennials accepted college debt as a part of life, but one in five[9] Gen Zers wish to avoid personal debt of *any* kind.

There is no security, no guarantee that your job will last; people rarely stay eighteen years in one job as I have with Skees Family Foundation, or forty years as my father did with Standard Register. There is no safety net of decent insurance or retirement plans, so workers feel far more isolated and stressed.

The workplace can, too often, provide no web of support, no integral system of mentors and cohorts to see you through the changes of time, talent, parenting, health issues, financial hardship, and life milestones. This rings true even more so in the era of COVID, when we work from behind face masks or online and solo.

As networked as this smaller world has become through instant online "connection," our careers and personal lives offer no guarantees for the future and no positive reviews of our efforts. It's as if each worker strives alone on a little boat in an increasingly lonely ocean.

The Surprising Shift in Gen Z's Views

Perhaps Gen Zers will shift their way of working back to being in-person — even if it is on-screen, across space — sharing tea and stories about their gym workout or human-rights march last weekend, praising each other's efforts and inspiring one another to try harder, and creating a sense of community in profound and lasting work-relationships, one that will fulfill team members even as they build better products and services.

They resemble Boomers — their parents/ grandparents — in that they're earnest, hardworking, and driven by traditional views of success (money, education, career). However, this generation is also writing new rules that favor liberal — almost radical — viewpoints on things like race, gender, identity and sexuality.

"They have views that look a lot more like parents and grandparents, probably older generations, Gen X, in their attitudes, but then they have hyper-connectivity. It's sort of this intersection of mobile first, mobile connected but traditional views, traditional values," reports Jeff Fromm,[10] partner at Barkley advertising agency and author of *Marketing to Millennials*[11], which in conjunction with FutureCast did a study on Gen Z. Pointing out that Gen Zers grew up "post-digital," without the need to adapt to technology, they conclude that this is a generation of "old souls in young bodies."

Also opposite of Millennials, 63 percent of whom believe career success depends on luck, 69 percent[12] of Gen Zers attribute success to hard work.

Who's in This Book, and Why

As we dug into our research, we found substantial material on how to *market* to Generation Z.

Why? Because they're a goldmine: the largest consumer base on Earth. However — partly due to their youth, which means most are just embarking on their careers — slim pickings turned up on the topic of Gen Z *at work*.

So, we decided to ask Gen Zers directly: *Who are you, what are your dream jobs, and where are you now in relation to those dreams?*

I realize that, given my rather advanced age (I'm in my fifties), I've been listening to "job stories" longer than Gen Zers have been alive. Hundreds[13] of laborers, farmers, teachers, artists, designers, factory workers, activists, accountants, and others of all ages and nationalities have shared with me what it's really like to do the work they do.

Also, because of my work with a nonprofit[14] whose mission is to create dignified jobs to end global poverty (training for/equal access to jobs with fair wages), I view a job as far more than a way to earn a paycheck.

The Powerful Impact Our Jobs Have on Our Wellbeing

Writing hundreds of interviews and articles about jobs — and now three books — has convinced me that they have the power to build or shatter our self-esteem and wellbeing. What we "do" deeply influences our personal identity; and what we earn ripples out far beyond our own bank accounts, into our families and communities, and even our nations' gross domestic product (GDP), a measure of national wealth.

If we don't have a job, our risk for both physical and mental illness skyrockets,[15] while our self-confidence plummets. Conversely, if everyone who wants to work and/or needs the income has empowered choices about what they do, our society will run like clockwork, with roads and buildings, hospitals and schools, entertainment and hospitality services, all well-equipped.

Work: The Universal Experience for People from All Walks of Life

What I discovered when listening to people's job stories is that they have the power to unite us; because *everyone* has, had, or will have a job.

We've all worked long hours without recognition, striven extra hard to meet a deadline, benefited from camaraderie among our coworkers, endured a horrible boss, and celebrated a promotion or raise. Despite our differences in gender, politics, culture and religion, sharing our job stories unites us as human beings.

What has surprised me in my work to support
job creation and document job stories is the way that
every single person I've interviewed has opened up to
share far more than what they do at work.

Humans are multidimensional, after all; we take
our whole selves with us to the office. Our family
dynamics, early trauma, romantic attractions, fears
and dreams, all come to work with us and impact our
workplace. Sometimes, we know our coworkers more
intimately than those at home. Always, we discover
our potential through the challenges, injustices, and
feedback that we get on the job.

What This Book Has Taught Me About Gen Z

Watching the members of Generation Z whom I know
and love in my personal life, I became intrigued by
the way they approach work. I wondered how they
would react to the gig economy, robotics, artificial
intelligence, über-rapidly developing technology, and
globalization.

Even for Gen Zers still in school, it seemed their
career choices could be paralyzingly complex and
the work-world frighteningly competitive. I wanted to
learn more — not just about them but from them.

Turns out, the results of our Gen Z survey aligned
with industry statistics on Gen Z (what makes you
unique and how you approach work), and provided
insight into where young people clock in right now, en
route to their career goals.

To Sanam and me, these (extra) "ordinary,"
unknown Gen Zers prove that anyone reading these
pages can aspire to and reach their dreams. To amplify

that message — and provide further inspiration — we've also highlighted Gen Zers in the media who've earned fortunes and fame, invented companies and products, and wielded influence and impact in their communities and far beyond.

BLM, Racial Justice, and Our World of Whiplash-Fast Change

Just before releasing this book, we added research and resources on how Gen Z deals with life during the COVID pandemic, how to network and job-hunt from home, and how Gen Zers like you have adapted to studying/working remotely or not at all.

We've also added a section on racial justice and Black Lives Matter (BLM), because second only to the coronavirus outbreak, Gen Z reports that the BLM movement is one of the most impactful events on their worldview; the vast majority (90 percent)[16] supports BLM protests. The power and influence of YOU, the largest portion of Earth's population and workforce, is also our brightest hope for the future.

Strive on,
Suzanne

Chapter 1: How Gen Z Works

As sixty-one million Gen Zers enter the workforce in the U.S. alone, what advantages and challenges do they face? What are their values and aspirations?

How We Define Generation Z

First of all, who *is* Generation Z?

You'll find disparity in the parameters of this generation, but this book defines Generation Z as people born between 1995-2015; that's currently everyone from preschool up to university, as well as the youngest professionals in the field.

Excepting the Preface, in which Gen Zer Sanam addresses her cohorts directly, we will use third-person pronouns. Moreover, out of respect for many Gen Zers' wish not to be pigeonholed into one gender or another, we will use the pronoun *they* rather than *she* or *he*.

Reading hundreds of articles and books to build a foundation of knowledge about this generation, we were shocked and dismayed to find condescending references everywhere — "for such a young person," "at the ripe old age of ___," "believe it or not" — dismissive qualifiers that undercut a Gen Zer's intelligence and accomplishments. We strove to weed out any such ageism. Let us know if we missed anything!

What People Call Generation Z

Nicknames for this generation:

- Generation Z/Gen Z
- Centennials
- iGen
- Founders
- Pivotals
- Digital Natives
- The Action Generation
- Throwback Generation
- Zoomers

For our purposes, we've adopted the abbreviated "Gen Z" and call members "Gen Zers."

Fast, Savvy and No B.S.

They have an infamous attention span of just eight seconds[17] — less than a goldfish. Often they're on five devices at once, compared with Millennials on three. Conversely, because they've grown up digital, they're much more savvy about knowing when they're being fed "fake news."

Gen Zers have "a fast-paced, highly selective and decisive filter — something that marketers have never encountered before," report Gen Zers Connor Blakely and serial entrepreneur Deep Patel in *The Huffington Post*. Gen Zers have a built-in bullshit detector; they bring and demand authenticity everywhere they go.

What the Statistics Show[18]

- Powerful consumers: At 40 percent, largest consumer base on the planet
- Ethnically diverse: 47 percent in U.S. are non-white
- Nomophobes: 95 percent have access to a smartphone
- Digital natives: 50 percent spend ten hours a day online
- 67 percent prefer to do their shopping in physical stores
- Very social: 71 percent watch three hours of YouTube videos of other humans each day, and 39 percent admit their self-esteem is directly influenced by social media
- Impactful: 80 percent choose brands that are ecofriendly and socially responsible

Another study recently conducted by Response Media finds that Gen Zers …

- Showcase their aspirational selves on Instagram
- Share real-life moments on Snapchat
- Get the news on Twitter or TikTok
- Glean information from Facebook

And their preferred social media sites differ even between younger and older Gen Zers, as shown in this chart by YPulse.[19]

Their Favorite Social Platforms to Use Now	
13-18-year-olds	19-25-year-olds
1. Instagram	1. Instagram
2. YouTube	2. TikTok
3. Snapchat	3. Snapchat
4. TikTok	4. Facebook
5. Twitter	5. YouTube

Source: YPulse Survey n=1000 ages 13-39 | April 2020

Many members of Generation Z grew up with the first Black U.S. President. Equality and diversity are important issues for them now, just as they were during Barack Obama's presidency. In a study,[20] 72 percent of Gen Z members said racial equality is the most important issue today, while 64 percent added gender equality and 48 percent sexual orientation equality.

Forbes[21] cites 75 percent of Gen Zers as not viewing college as imperative to building a strong education. When they seek out employment, they rank diversity, good management, and job fluidity (ability to fulfill varying roles) as most vital. Money may not motivate their career choices, but more than any preceding generation (81 percent), it causes them stress.

Infographics Show Ways Gen Z Is Different

The graphics[22] in this chapter, used with permission from the author Abby Quillen,[23] sum up the demographics of Generation Z:

MEET
GENERATION Z

 BORN **BETWEEN 1997** AND THE **EARLY 2010s**

MAKES UP **25.9%** OF THE **U.S. POPULATION**

49% IDENTIFY AS NON-WHITE

COMPARED TO

44% OF MILLENIALS

40% OF GEN X

28% OF BOOMERS

98%	92%	50%
OWN A **SMARTPHONE**	HAVE A **DIGITAL FOOTPRINT**	ARE CONNECTED ONLINE FOR **10 HOURS A DAY**

70%	40%	80%
WATCH MORE THAN **TWO HOURS OF YOUTUBE** EACH DAY	SAY **THEY'RE ADDICTED** TO THEIR PHONES	FEEL **DISTRESSED WHEN KEPT AWAY** FROM PERSONAL ELECTRONIC DEVICES

SOURCES:
mediakix.com
huffingtonpost.com
forbes.com
blog.globalwebindex.com

MILLENNIALS vs. GENERATION Z

MILLENNIALS

GENERATION Z

Born between about
1980 & **1996**

Born between about
1997 & **2010s**

B MOST WERE RAISED BY
BABY BOOMERS

X MOST WERE RAISED BY
GEN XERS

 GREW UP DURING
AN **ECONOMIC BOOM**

GREW UP DURING
A **RECESSION**

 TEND TO BE **IDEALISTIC**

TEND TO BE **PRAGMATIC**

 FOCUSED ON HAVING
EXPERIENCES

FOCUSED ON
SAVING MONEY

 MOBILE **PIONEERS**

MOBILE **NATIVES**

 PREFER BRANDS THAT
SHARE THEIR VALUES

PREFER BRANDS THAT
FEEL AUTHENTIC

 PREFER **FACEBOOK**
& INSTAGRAM

 PREFER **SNAPCHAT**
& INSTAGRAM

SOURCES:
businessinsider.com
thedrum.com
thinkwithgoogle.com
wpengine.netdna-cdn.com

GENERATION Z
IN THE WORKPLACE

Percentage who prefer **face-to-face conversation**

72%

Percentage who prefer their **own workspace**

69%

Percentage who expect to **work harder than previous generations**

77%

Percentage who want to have **multiple roles** in an organization

75%

Percentage who say **equality is the most important cause** they want their employer to support

36%

Percentage who believe **racial equality is the most important issue** today

72%

Percentage who'd prefer to work in a **midsize or large company**

80%

GENERATION Z
IN THE WORKPLACE

Two greatest aspirations after college:

TO BE FINANCIALLY STABLE AND FIND A DREAM JOB

Two most important factors in a job:

EMPOWERING WORK CULTURE AND POTENTIAL FOR CAREER GROWTH

The two most important skills for succeeding in the workplace according to Gen Z:

COMMUNICATION AND PROBLEM SOLVING

SOURCES:
inc.com
diversitybestpractices.com
adeccousa.com
blog.evan-jenkins.com
medium.com

The Surprising Qualities of Gen Z

David and Jonah Stillman's book *Gen Z @ Work: How the Next Generation Is Transforming the Workplace*[24] lists some unique findings regarding Gen Z. Granted, their focus is on how to *market* to Generation Z; but we find that such qualities as *realistic, DIY, FOMO,* and *weconomist* show up in many other aspects of Gen Zers' lives as well.

1. **Phigital:** The line between the physical and digital worlds for Gen Z hasn't just been blurred; it's been completely eliminated. 91 percent of Gen Zers say that a company's

technological sophistication would influence their decision to accept a position with a firm.

2. **Hyper-Custom:** Gen Zers have always worked hard at identifying and tailoring their brands for the world to know. From job titles to career paths, the pressure to customize has been turned up! Some 56 percent of of Gen Zers want to write their own job descriptions.

3. **Realistic:** Growing up with skeptical Gen X parents in the aftermath of 9/11 and the Great Recession has created in Gen Z a very pragmatic mindset when it comes to preparing for the future.

4. **FOMO:** Gen Zers suffer from an intense fear of missing out on anything. The good news is that they will stay on top of all trends; the bad news is that they will worry they're not moving ahead fast enough.

5. **Weconomists:** From Uber to Airbnb, Gen Zers have only known a world with a shared economy. They will push to break down internal and external silos like never before.

6. **DIY:** Gen Z is the do-it-yourself generation. Its fierce, independent nature will collide head-on with so many of the collaborative cultures that Millennials have fought for.

7. **Driven:** With parents who drilled into them that there are winners and there are losers, this demographic is one motivated group: 72 percent of Gen Zers say they are competitive with people doing the same job.

The One Thing Gen Zers Want Most at Work

Another author, Jessica Stillman (not related to David and Jonah, cited above), reports in *Inc.* magazine[25] on a new study of 11 million workplace comments, showing that "Everyone wants to be paid decently, treated with respect, and have a life outside the office."

But not for Gen Z: They want one thing above all else.

Gen Zers differ in that they look for companies that take a stand on political issues and are engaged with the world outside their company. They don't want to be part of a company that's just about profits.

Gen Zers, "raised in a time when the effects of climate change are making weekly headlines, care deeply about the world around them," Stillman says.

And more Gen Zers than any other generation (by a landslide) are likely to make employment decisions based on whether they agree with the stances and values of their employer — both the company and their boss.

Not Their Parents' or Grandparents' Work-World

Our survey[26] revealed vivid ways in which this generation differs from their predecessors. We've grouped respondents' stories into similar experiences, as follows.

Kyle

Twenty-three-year-old transgender male Kyle works in Tampa, Florida, as a lube tech for Hyundai, changing the oil in cars, rotating tires, checking air filters, and refilling windshield and coolant fluids.

Striving toward his goal of becoming an auto mechanic, he's an exception in noting that his parents and grandparents all worked in "physically relaxed" desk jobs, while he "loves the people" and the "hands-on, physically demanding work" of automotive repair.

Michael

We heard from far more Gen Zers who expect the opposite.

For example, Michael from Taylor, Michigan, says, "I expect my labor to be mental as opposed to the manual labor that my parents and grandparents are engaged in.

"Moreover, I foresee myself in a workplace that is constantly changing and not doing a job that is repetitive from day to day (e.g., law as opposed to factory work)."

Siddhant

Twenty-one-year-old Siddhant notes, "Everyone in my family has been service-based, [such as] in the jewelry business or serving for the Army, but I am trying to serve in healthcare for people."

His dream job is to be a pediatric cardiologist, and he's on his way now as an unpaid intern at his local hospital in Los Angeles, California.

He feels the weight of great expectations from his parents to become a doctor and earn a lot of money. Majoring in biology and minoring in Spanish and Japanese, Siddhant wants to coach soccer on the side.

Mia

Mia, a 20-year-old from San Antonio, Texas, says, "I hope to truly love what I do" — unlike her mother, who quit her teaching job to raise her children, and her father, a lawyer who wishes he were a teacher.

Marie

Marie, a 23-year-old cinema concessions clerk in Newark, New Jersey, wants to own a business someday and believes that, unlike her parents' and grandparents' generations, women now can "be the boss."

Her biggest obstacle is her student loans. Virtually all of our survey respondents have felt stress and limitations due to academic debt.

Daniel

Seventeen-year-old Daniel (a woman) from the biblical town of Beer Sheva, Israel, dreams of being a lawyer or FBI agent — something her parents and grandparents would never have aspired to be.

"It is my dream, and I plan to achieve it," she resolves.

She currently works in the office of a summer camp. "I am also responsible for other logistical stuff, calling people, making sure they paid for the camp, calling other candidates to fill out an application, organizing everything," she says.

She shares what it's like to be on her side of her company's outreach. "My phone is constantly going crazy with emails, calls and texts. I don't like being serious all the time at my job. I also don't like it when people don't answer my phone calls …

"Don't hang up in my face — that's plain rude, and it is my job to be nice to you. Don't yell at me for things that are out of my control, because sometimes I really want to help but they don't even give me a chance.

"With all that said, I love my job, it's fun, and I feel really professional working in an actual office."

Constant Adaptation to New Technology

Parker

Gen Zers face a work-world their parents could not even have imagined.

For example, 21-year-old Parker works full time for a nonprofit organization, The Representation Project, as the manager of the "Youth Media Lab," a new kind of social media platform for activists ages 14 to 24.

Her role entails marketing for the app, moderating the app, managing, hiring, and facilitating app

"Ambassadors," and implementing new strategies. She makes $20 per hour.

She says, "My work for this job differs day to day." When her parents were starting off, there were no such platforms as apps and social media.

Sydney

Sydney, from Rye, New York, says that "new technological advances in the workplace produce great shifts. I want to pursue music, an industry that is rapidly changing and morphing to the new advancements being made in streaming."

Chase

Twenty-year-old Chase in Santa Cruz, California, cites advanced technology as what will set her career apart from her predecessors.

Her dream job is photography, and her path toward that is in food service. She started off as a runner for a Hawaiian restaurant and now works as a hostess/busser at a fine dining restaurant on a golf course, which hosts the sort of weddings and special events she hopes one day to photograph.

For now, she makes minimum wage. Chase says, "I love the social aspect of it and meeting people from all over the world and forming a team with my coworkers.

"It is very hard work, and going out of your way to meet peoples' needs can be challenging but also a good skill. I have learned many things while working in the restaurant industry.

"I have learned how to manage my time, to have patience, to multitask and be flexible, that communication is key, and that people can be *very* demanding."

Shaked

This 16-year-old summer camp counselor in Israel expects her career to be "way more connected to social media, way more global, and very fast-changing and unique."

Her current job "is the most exhausting yet rewarding experience," she reflects. "I get to work with kids every day.

"I learn a lot from them, and I can always see how good kids are on their basic level. They are also very needy and require full attention and dedication.

"I love my job. I have a job environment that respects me and my rights and is made out of people my age that I can relate to and get help from."

Working from the Ground Up Toward the Dream Goal

Ariel

Eighteen-year-old Ariel from Boston dreams of a job "where I make everything I need to survive (grow my own food, provide my own energy, sell produce on the side to buy things I need) ...

"That would be the ultimate and unattainable dream."

She says she's got a long way to go from the job she just quit: "I last worked in a restaurant as a hostess. I made $13/hour; everything about it sucked."

Melissa

Melissa, a 20-year-old Ulta beauty advisor working in Huntington Beach, California, will be the first in her family to graduate college.

She hopes to make more money and work as a nutritionist, but for now she enjoys "being surrounded by all things beauty" in a "fun and easy environment."

Will

This 19-year-old video production intern in Redwood City, California, notes, "As occupations become more specialized, I feel like it is harder to know where I will end up than it might have been for my parents."

Currently he's in his final year of high school and earning money on the side as a front-desk clerk at a climbing gym.

"The worst part of my job," he laments, "is probably cleaning the hair out of the bathroom drains at the end of the day; but I feel like I've become a little numb to that at this point."

Joanna

Twenty-four-year-old Joanna from Ft. Smith, Arizona, is working her way through graduate school with a career goal of guidance counseling.

Her current role is as a full-time teller at a credit union making $13 per hour, and for Joanna, it's all about the people.

"What I love about my current job are the interactions I get to have with our members," she says.

"I love making personal connections with them as well as helping them the best I can with their accounts. What I do hate, however, are rude members. Members who think they are entitled whenever there is an issue and refuse to work with us."

Becka

Becka, a 23-year-old from Michigan, started off as a gas station pizza cook.

She feels stuck in her current job in manufacturing and unable to work toward her dream job of editing and marketing books for independently published authors.

"I spend more time daydreaming about the side gig than actually working on it, as most of my awake time is stuck being present at something completely irrelevant to what I would rather be doing," she says.

She sees a direct correlation between her unfulfilling job and the contribution she wishes to make to the world.

"I'm a girl stuck in an environment she hates: one that doesn't care about flexible hours, employee development, or even rewarding us when we do a good job.

"Who I *want* to be is a woman who gets to work remotely, have no income limit, do work that I love, and do it with honesty and genuine compassion. I want to help people help themselves, so they can achieve the same happiness I so desperately crave in my everyday life."

Instinct for Entrepreneurism

The generation after Millennials grew up during the recession, witnessing the collapse of the housing market and their parents losing their jobs.

They're under no illusions that there is such a thing as a completely secure job. As Jacob Morgan, author of *The Future of Work*,[27] says, "Job security is a complete myth, as is long-term employment. Companies lay off employees in droves ... by the thousands! They just make sweeping cuts when they need to."

The average employee tenure is under five years and for millennials, it's under three years, says Morgan. Another source cites 0.8-1.5[28] years as being the average length of time Gen Zers remain in a job.

Kian

Gen Zers seem to have innate entrepreneurial zest. For example, 20-year-old Kian, who dreams of being a fashion editor, already works toward that goal while enrolled in college. First, he served as a marketing intern for makeup company SEPHORA, and now he contracts out his own design projects for his friend's swimsuit line.

Jazmine

Jazmine, a 23-year-old from Detroit, Michigan, didn't wait for anyone to bestow her dream job of being an executive director for a nonprofit organization.

She launched Urban Outdoor Outreach[29] in 2016. Her mission is to introduce urban youth to the transformative powers of the outdoors and close the "racial and economic 'adventure gap'" to benefit not only the youth themselves, but also American conservation.

"I manage everything for the organization from funding, to programming, to filing tax paperwork," she says.

"Right now, I do not earn anything. The top aspect of my job is that I am doing what I love and helping others.

"I hate that my job is so demanding, and even in cases where the maximum effort is put in (such as with grant writing) there are sometimes no returns."

There's a certain *hustle* energy about this generation; rather than feeling daunted at the lack of security and benefits in the workplace, they thrive on making their own rules, schedules and benefits.

Drive Toward Impact Over Money

Sam

Our survey respondents ranked *stability* and *making an impact* above salary and fame.

Unlike many of his cohorts, 21-year-old Sam strives for fame above all else — perhaps in part because of his chosen field, screenwriting.

Currently, he works as an assistant to the CEO of an entertainment company in Los Angeles.

"The job oftentimes is stressful and requires long hours," he says. He makes $18 per hour ($1,000/week) and loves the people he works with, of whom he says "I've found to be crucial" to his wellbeing at work.

Sydney

Gen Zers view themselves as global citizens.

Many might agree with 19-year-old Sydney from Brisbane, Australia, who says, "I want to work as an international teacher. I do not want to stay at home. I want to live in different cities and see the world.

"I want to travel and be able to say that I wasn't born in the same city I grew up and died in."

For her, work equals freedom. "I crave independence," she says, "and I know the first step to gaining this independence is getting a job."

Ella

Ella from New York City is 17 years old. So far, she's worked only in unpaid internships. Her number one goal is to make an impact, through politics, at the United Nations.

Kylene

Kylene from Birmingham, Alabama, dreams of becoming a psychologist to veterans.

"I want to help individuals be the best version of themselves," she says, ranking "making an impact" as her highest career goal.

Facing Age Discrimination

Donna

One obstacle Gen Zers face is inherent in the way some coworkers perceive them because of their age.

Twenty-one-year-old Donna works two jobs en route to her dream of being an interior designer: as a retail associate, assisting customers as they shop and running the register as they check out; and as a design intern, shadowing and assisting two designers in deciding and planning interior spaces.

"I love the opportunities I am gaining from my two jobs," she says, "but also don't like how I am not taken very seriously at my internship because I am young and don't have much experience yet."

The Insecurity of the Gig Economy

Chloe

Their parents may have worked a side job or two to pay the rent and put food on the table, but Gen Z may begin and end their careers in the *gig* economy — that is, working as independent contractors for one or many firms, with no job security or benefits.

Chloe wants to be a partner at an accounting firm, but for now she works as a DoorDash driver.

Catering to companies and families when they order food on the app, she says, "I love the flexibility of picking my own hours, but I do *not* like how unorganized and how badly designed the system is for us.

"We often are underpaid," she complains, "because of an app flaw. They also lack a support center to deal with our issues.

"At the end of the day I make around $18/hour, but it comes with a lot of annoyance."

Working amid the flux of evolving technology, her generation will always experience firsthand the bugs that accompany new tech.

Chapter 2: "Ordinary" Gen Zers Building Extraordinary Careers

We surveyed *real* Gen Zers to discover what it's like to launch a career (with or without training or college courses) in today's world.

Our narrators hail from across the United States and around the world. They work in politics, retail, fashion design, education and pornography.

We're proud to highlight them here. We've listed these twenty rockstars in alphabetical order by their first names, so if your friend made it into this book, you can easily find them.

Catherine, 18, University Student

St. Andrews, Fife, Scotland, U.K.

My first job was as a barista, but my dream job would be anything that allows me to express my activism creatively (for example: ad agency, media company, etc.). I expect my career to be a lot more art- and technology-focused than the careers of my parents. My number one goal is stability, but making an impact is a close second for me.

Currently, I am a university student and do not have a job due to time constraints.

Previously, I worked as a behind-the-counter person and barista at a local bakery. I dealt with customer relations as well as the general wellbeing/cleanliness of the bakery. I worked three to four shifts a week for $11/hour. I mainly chose to work at this bakery in order to gain experience as well as to earn money for my future travels.

I believe my career path will head in a far different direction than the jobs I've previously held, but still believe they were important to the development of my career.

COVID Update: Last March, I had a job lined up to work as a waitress at a hotel restaurant. Due to the travel ban and my school going online, I left the U.K. and went back home to California, ultimately having to turn down the job. I haven't considered getting a job this summer due to concerns about COVID. I thought about getting a remote internship, but figured I was busy enough with work from the committees I joined at school.

Danielle, 26, TSA Officer for the Department of Homeland Security

Tampa, Florida, U.S.

I help protect the nation's transportation systems, especially in my home airport.

I earn approximately $33K a year. What I love about my job is that no two days are the same. I get to interact with people from different walks of life on a daily basis.

I also enjoy knowing that the work I'm doing is helping people travel with the assurance that they'll be safe flying from one destination to another.

Jasmin, 24, Crew Member at Trader Joe's
New York City, New York, U.S.

My career will be different from my parents' in that I will probably end up working for myself rather than for someone else.

I currently work at Trader Joe's in the Lower East Side of Manhattan. As a crew member I work every section of the store and process transactions. I earn $17.35 an hour.

I love the company culture and the benefits that Trader Joe's offers. I dislike having to work with difficult customers while having to keep a smile on my face.

COVID Update: At the beginning of 2020, I was working six to seven days a week between a full-time job as an urban farmer in a controlled-environment hydroponic farm, and a part-time job as a crew member at Trader Joe's.

In May of this year, after two months of working remotely doing research and online learning for my position at the farm, I was let go.

Fortunately, I was able to return full-time to Trader Joe's — although that also meant increasing my potential exposure to COVID-19 as an essential worker.

During the weeks following my return to TJ's full-time, I felt very hopeless about securing another agriculture job, considering the many years of experience needed and degrees I do not have. I even questioned how the urban agriculture industry as a whole would survive this period of time.

Recently, however, I was offered a part-time position working for the Hydroponic Team of an award-winning nonprofit organization that builds hydroponic labs in schools. I will be back to working six days a week to make ends meet and make my own [career-related] dreams come true.

”

Josiah, 19, Gap Year

Astoria, Oregon, U.S.

The unknown factors of life that came from the COVID pandemic gave me the courage to take a leap of faith and do something that I never would've seen myself doing before.

I knew I didn't wanna stay in the craziness of the COVID-era education system, so I decided to take a year off and go live on a farm in Hawaii!

I also decided to use all the free time from COVID to self-improve, stay off of social media, and teach myself guitar — which is now a pretty big part of my life.

I understand that many of those things do come from a place of privilege, but I'm still very thankful for the opportunities that I've been able to capitalize on for myself during this time.

Kamrie, 24, Freelance Real Estate Photographer and Stager

Brooklyn, New York, U.S.

Kamrie ranks upward mobility and making money as her two top career priorities. However, she believes that her career will differ sharply from those of her parents, "because I'm actually pursuing my dream career rather than simply being after a good job that pays the bills.

Currently, I work as a freelance floor-plan artist for a company that provides services (photography, floor plans, virtual staging, videos, etc.) for real estate agents for all their property needs.

Simply put, I meet brokers at the address of their listing(s) and then draft the floor plan for the space. How much I am paid is dependent on two things: How many floor plans I draw during a pay period, and how many rooms are at a specific listing.

This means that my paychecks are never the same and are dependent upon the real estate season. Some paychecks can be upwards of $3,000 — while during the slow season, which is around the end/start of year holidays, paychecks can be as low as $200.

What I love about my job is the flexibility. I can take off whenever I want without having to get approved and I can make myself unavailable during specific points in the day if that was my desire.

Another thing I love is that I get to travel to many different neighborhoods and go into homes/apartments that are amazing and sometimes worth millions of dollars ... literally places that you would only see on television or that someone would never get to experience in their life.

However, with good comes bad; so, some places I go to you wouldn't want to walk in if your life depended on it (usually foreclosures).

As a result of my position being considered freelance, I don't have an office. This means I spend my days outside and I am constantly exposed to the elements. The burning sun, the pouring rain, and the harshest snow are all things I have to be willing to deal with in order to do this job.

The last thing I hate about the job is the fact that it is a freelance position. That means no benefits from the company, since I am not an employee, as well as having to pay money back during tax season.

99

Kelly, 17, Office Admin for Hulu

New York City, New York, U.S.

Kelly from New York City, New York, may be only seventeen years old, but she makes $22 an hour as a temporary contractor for Hulu, filling in as a workplace experience assistant during an employee's maternity leave.

She's essentially an office admin, responsible for all the facilities and office-wide events. She maintains all food and office supplies and provides assistance wherever it's needed.

I love being helpful and essentially do not hate anything about my job — just that it can be very time- and energy-consuming.

Kristen, 24, International Facility Manager

Bilbao, Spain

I work for an international company in a department dedicated to Facility Management. I studied management engineering at university, and mostly what I do is arranging the execution of very varied projects (construction work, equipment maintenance and repairs, office services delivery, reception, cleaning, security, etc.) for private companies.

What I most like from my job is that I get the chance to travel around the country visiting clients, and that I have earned a lot of responsibility.

What I most hate is that every client request is *always* urgent, and since there is a lack of staff in my department, I cannot respond as good and fast as I think it should be done. Moreover, I feel like I need more training from the company in this field.

My parents both worked in manual labor jobs. I believe my career will be more intellectually based.

Kristina, 18, Restaurant Waitress and Hostess

San Mateo, California, U.S.

I'm a waitress and hostess in a restaurant where I've been working since I was 15. I make $15/hour.

While it's nice having the spending money while I'm in school, the best part of the job for me is getting to interact with so many kinds of people — including those I normally wouldn't get a chance to know in my day-to-day life.

Having coworkers from different age groups and ethnic and financial backgrounds has opened my eyes to what lies outside my own geographical community.

Befriending everyone from the undocumented immigrants in the kitchen to the young single mom working sixteen-hour days, and honing my communication skills and patience with customers,

I've gotten the opportunity to practice unconditional kindness and acceptance. I wouldn't change anything about the job, if I'm being honest.

I know it's not much income for an adult paying bills in the Bay Area, but for me it's the perfect space to use a part of my brain that I don't get to use at school or with my friends.

Even though I won't work in such an environment forever, starting my life in the workforce with a minimum wage job has been all about helping me see what lies outside the world of the one percent.

I want to give my life for the betterment of the world rather than for my own financial gain. Also, I want to contribute to a global community rather than just my own little bubble.

COVID Update: For the past few years I have worked at a local restaurant as a server and host, and this summer I was planning on doing the same.

However, the restaurant industry has been hit incredibly hard by the pandemic and mine in particular has had to rely on the loyalty of its employees just to stay afloat.

All of us are working three or more jobs for the same wage as before. For example, I not only manage the takeout counter but have also been doing inventory and accounting, dishwashing, and prep for the kitchen. I can feel how stressed and overworked my boss and the other employees are every time I go to work.

I'm very grateful to have a job at all right now, but it's hard to watch my coworkers worry about their livelihoods when there's no immediate solution to their struggles.

Lana, 19, Online Tutor

New York City, New York, U.S.

I was supposed to do a program through my school called DukeEngage, which is a program that places students in communities worldwide for a minimum of eight weeks.

Throughout their experience, students have the opportunity to work with local partners to address community issues and learn about social change. My program was in Cape Town, South Africa, where I was supposed to work at the Scalabrini Centre of Cape Town.

Fortunately for me, they made DukeEngage an online program and I was still able to work for Scalabrini, online from the United States, and have an engaging experience. I've made curriculums, tutored students over WhatsApp, and served as a [remote] TA for multiple classes.

Although I would have much preferred being in-person and getting to know the people I was working with, my experience has still been insightful and positive, and I feel like I'm part of a community.

Matthew, 22, Electrical Engineering Intern

Cincinnati, Ohio, U.S.

I currently work as an electrical engineering intern at a company in Monroe, Ohio, called NuWaves. I enjoy getting to solve problems that no one else has solved before.

Because it's a small company, I get to not only work on new problems but many aspects of those problems. I currently make ~$18/hour. That wage is a good starting point for when you do not have any experience in the industry.

I'm starting to get into a field called Digital Signal Processing (DSP) and that is a *very* math-heavy field and one that not a lot of people get into.

You have all new problems to solve. Since everything is done digitally, people can sell the solution to problems as soon as they have it completed and working.

The downside of my work is that we have significant interactions with the government, so there's a ton of paperwork and bureaucracy that goes along with those contracts.

My parents and grandparents had more "traditional" jobs, and currently I am going down a very new path of engineering. If that ever fails or if I decide that I do not want to do it any longer, I'll probably go become a mountain-climbing guide.

COVID Update: I still expect to be graduating in less than a year. By that time, I hope things will return to normal, but am preparing and planning for things to still be closed. So as far as a job goes with that, I am focusing my search for jobs that can be done either remotely or in-person.

Right now I am still working. I currently have two jobs, one full-time and one part-time. My full-time job is 90 percent online and the part-time job is about 50/50. The part-time job includes a good amount of manufacturing that cannot really be done at home.

Given this outbreak, I think there will be a significant shift towards online work. Even if the majority of jobs do not begin to work completely from home, I think employers will allow people to work from home one or more days a week and not have that be part of a "benefits package."

With my career I do not see a large delta in what I planned on originally and what I believe is achievable now, simply because I am able to do so much of it online as opposed to in the office.

99

Michael L., 21, Airframe Mechanic for the U.S. Marine Corps

Kailua, Hawaii, U.S.

Michael got his start in construction work, and now he's already working in his dream job as a "non-destructive inspector" managing automated systems.

I work as an airframe mechanic, repairing structural, hydraulic, and tire assemblies on multiple different aircraft platforms and support equipment.

I am also qualified as an aeronautical welder and non-destructive inspector, utilizing radiography, ultrasonic, and a variety of other inspection methods to detect defects in components.

I earn roughly $80,000 annually. This includes the cost of medical/dental, life insurance, housing allowance, cost of living allowance, etc. I love my job because it is hands-on, and each day is a new problem I get to solve.

Michael T., 19, Legislative Aide to State Senator

Taylor, Michigan, U.S.

 My dream job is to be a partner at a law firm. Meanwhile, I work as a legislative aide to a state senator in my home state of Michigan.

Within my role, I am in charge of researching policy, taking notes of all meetings that the senator attends, assisting constituents with any issues that our office has the ability to handle, and many other responsibilities.

This job — much like my dream job — is ever-changing and entirely mental. I love it because every day is a fresh start and every task is different from the last. It never gets monotonous.

However, it does have its problems. I'm employed at a salaried wage that equates to roughly $16/hour, and surely any college student dreams of this type of position — both for reasons of pay and resume boosting.

Yet, most people who fill these positions have graduated from college and are in need of a career that can support them as financially independent adults (usually with a significant amount of student loans).

This demonstrates the statistic of college-educated adults that are compensated below the median income of the country. This is disconcerting for a few reasons.

Everyone is expected to be significantly competent in a number of difficult skills (e.g., research, interpersonal skills, speech writing, and political maneuvering). The job requirements mixed with the emotional burden that the job can carry — as politics is inherently emotional — is usually not reflected in the compensation that myself and my colleagues receive.

And lastly, there are many times when we're beholden to people and ideas that we do not support. In the same way that most workers in any field are asked to do tasks they do not want to, we are, too.

But when we have political disagreements with those who have the power to enact policy (the elected officials), we have no choice but to assist in the carrying out of that which we may wholeheartedly disagree.

That is not to say the job is entirely bad, though. It's truly exhilarating to be hands-on with fighting for political change, to see my ideas valued in a political setting at such a young age, and to help solve issues for people that need it most.

I expect my labor to be mental as opposed to the manual labor that my parents and grandparents are engaged in. Moreover, I foresee myself in a workplace that is constantly changing and not doing a job that is repetitive from day to day; e.g., law as opposed to factory work.

"

Morgan, 22, Civil Engineering Intern

Cincinnati, Ohio, U.S.

Because I am the first engineer that my family has seen, I have no one to really ask professional questions to.

She enrolled in her local university's co-op program to gain access to relevant professional work while still an undergraduate — and she's worked for Procter & Gamble, Marathon Petroleum, and The Kleinger's Group (a small civil design firm).

I love the project management aspect of my job, as it allows me to utilize my technical knowledge on a variety of topics, along with interacting with contractors and building relationships with people.

My least favorite part of the job is probably the culture of the business, as everyone (including myself) is doing their best to climb the ranks, and although I am very competitive in nature, it gets tiring at times.

Pilar, 24, Dietetic Technician at an Eating Disorder Clinic

Los Angeles, California, U.S.

Unlike my parents' jobs, my job requires a Bachelor's (and soon Master's) degree. The salary is higher and the benefits are better. My career is not physically laborious like theirs.

Right now, I work as a Dietetic Technician at an Eating Disorder Treatment Center. I help individuals recover and re-mend their relationship with their food and their bodies.

I earn a little over minimum wage (I have to learn how to ask for a raise!). I also speak out against diet culture and create awareness of weight bias and "fatphobia."

On the side, I am a yoga teacher. I deliver donation-based yoga classes in underserved communities (primarily Latinx) in hopes to help gain body and mind trust and allow them accessibility to modes of wellness.

Rachel, 23, Hospital Employee Orientation Trainer

New York City, New York, U.S.

Rachel, who lives in New Jersey and works in New York City, does onboarding for employees at a major hospital, making around $50,000 per year.

I essentially do all parts of the pre-employment process, from background check, scheduling physicals, credentialing, etc., up to an individual's first day of work.

What I love most is having the freedom to work independently with collaborative efforts here and there. It can be stressful at times since there's so much to keep up with, but that keeps me on my toes.

She's the first in her family to earn both college and graduate degrees and expects to reach CEO level in her career.

Renn, 23, Nursing Home Activities Director

Walla Walla, Washington, U.S.

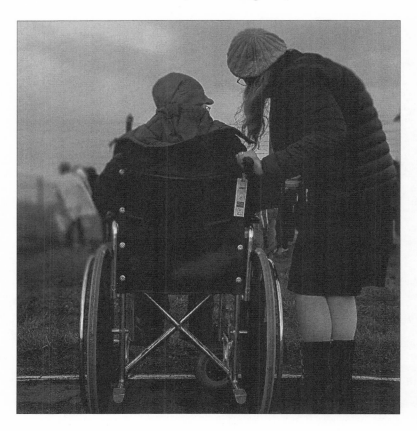

Since graduating college, I have worked in an assisted living and long-term care facility in the activities department, coordinating and leading both group and individual activities for over two hundred seniors.

I also work part-time as a nursing assistant, helping residents with bathing, dressing, toileting, feeding, eating, etc. By working both roles, I am learning how to care for residents' physical and emotional needs.

I earn minimum wage, which is $12/hour in Washington State.

Working in this environment is simultaneously rewarding and heartbreaking.

My favorite part of the job is the exchange between my own vibrant youth and the residents' calm wisdom and lived experience. Both parties benefit from this beautiful exchange, and the connections I have made fill me with so much love and joy.

The hardest aspect of my job is having to confront death and mortality on a daily basis. Each day I go in to work knowing a conversation with a resident might be my last. While this is undoubtedly challenging, I am grateful to be learning how to accept loss and change.

COVID Update: I'm currently unemployed — I recently moved cities (from Walla Walla, Washington to Portland, Oregon) and decided to take a few months off while settling in.

Based on my prior work experience and the need for essential workers during COVID-19, the job market currently available to me mainly consists of caring for people and health-oriented positions.

Over the next few years (while navigating the effects of the pandemic), I hope to pursue a variety of different work, volunteer, and travel opportunities so as to find a future career well suited for me.

"

Siddhant, 21, Hospital Intern

Los Angeles, California, U.S.

The way I see it, my career will be way different from my parents' and grandparents'. So far, everyone has been service based — e.g., in the jewelry business or serving in the army — but I hope to go into healthcare.

My number one career priority is making money.

I am not currently working anywhere, but I am interning at a hospital as I'm trying to become a doctor.

Due to the pressure of my parents, I am pursuing the track of a med student, but what I wanted to do was learn different languages and teach soccer.

Regardless, I am majoring in biology, minoring in Japanese, and studying Spanish. I am satisfied with my life.

Talia, 18, Lifeguard

Denver, Colorado, U.S.

This summer I was planning on working at my [community] pool, but I wasn't sure if it would end up opening.

Per the CDC guidelines, the pool opened but with heavy restrictions (no more than fifty people, no pool toys, no food or drink, masks except in the water).

Last summer, we would hit capacity with 300 people often, all toys and floats were allowed, and the tables and chairs were all open and available.

Now, to go to the pool people have to make reservations online, but it's so busy because everyone is trying to get out of their house.

The pool is also one of the best coronavirus options because it's outside, and the chlorine helps kill bacteria. It's really interesting as a staff member because I see regulars from last year that I used to interact with personally and often; however, now I cannot.

It's been an incredibly different experience working at the pool, but I'm lucky to have been able to have a job right now.

Tessa, 22, Grocery Store Clerk

Lexington, Kentucky, U.S.

No matter what I do, I've learned I'm happier when I get to work outside all day. I'm not saying my parents don't get to spend much time outside, but both of their jobs require being inside for most of the day.

I'm currently working at Wilson's Grocery & Meat in Lexington, Kentucky. Everyone who works there knows how to do everything required to keep the store running day-to-day.

Recently, my focus has been on inventory. I make orders to suppliers and go to other stores when it's cheaper (Costco, Aldi, etc.). I do this in addition to the tasks everyone does, like making sandwiches, selling meats, manning the register, cleaning, etc. I make $10.50/hour.

I love my job because most of the people I work with are very genuine and easy to work with. Plus, the owners are the people that my mom nannies for and they live right across the street, so I get to see them and their kids a lot.

Most of the time it's fun, but like every job, it has its downsides. Sometimes you get rude customers that degrade you and your coworkers every time they walk in.

Overall, I'm happy enough that I'm not actively looking for a new job.

Theodore, 24, Pornographic Webcam Model

Philadelphia, Pennsylvania, U.S.

I've worked many low-wage jobs since the age of sixteen. This has taken a huge toll on my mental and physical health.

This is the only job for which I meet the requirements where I can make a living wage and be treated with respect at work. But it's cost me the respect of my family in return.

It's worth it not to wonder where my next meal is coming from, unlike most of my college graduate peers.

I've watched all of my friends struggle to get a degree and go into debt; yet most of them have never used their degree, and still work low-wage jobs with no benefits.

I'm trying to do better for myself and adjust to the system ... but in doing that society looks down on me for not being willing to starve, struggle, and in the end still fail.

Chapter 3: Dream Jobs

Who's in This Chapter?

What does it take to land one's dream job at any age? Moreover, what inherent qualities do these dream-job attainers have that allow them to surpass the goals of their parents, grandparents, and often everyone around them, before they sprout their first gray hair?

We peered far beyond our home- and dorm-room offices, from here in California to all around the world, studying Gen Zers who've achieved and surpassed their dream jobs.

Initially, we found mostly YouTube stars, makeup and fashion mavens, Disney progeny and Kardashian-type heirs. However, that's just the skim of the headlines.

Digging deeper, we easily found one hundred American and global outliers in every field, from sports to music, engineering to food. Name an industry and chances are you'll find Gen Zers making their mark in it. Why?

How Did They Get There?

Gen Zers generally get things done. They are not waiting for anyone to hand them an opportunity. Their inventive and creative bent predisposes them to seek out new ways to get stuff done and find new forms and formats that can make the world a safer, sillier, prettier, funnier, more efficient, more equitable, and cleaner place.

Note that we've loosely categorized these dream-jobbers by industry, although several span more than one. To help you find them easily, they're listed alphabetically by their first name. We've included a few Millennials as well, based on the age they were when they launched their audacious ventures.

Stay tuned, as most of these dream-jobbers have found the grit to keep going through time. Unless otherwise noted, dream-job stories are culled from articles in *Business News Daily*[30], Due.com[31], *Entrepreneur*[32], and entries in Biography.com, Crunchbase, LinkedIn, TheFamousPeople.com, IMDb, Medium.com, Says.com, and Wikipedia. See the "Sources" section at the back of the book for further details as well as photograph credits.

We chose just a few superstars to represent each career category. If you don't find your favorite Gen Z celebrity or role model here, please jump onto our Instagram[33] or website[34] and tell us about them!

As with any slice of the population, this chapter contains a few individuals who perhaps see themselves as rare and uniquely gifted. However, the majority of Gen Zers profiled here have stated clearly that anyone can do this, and that all it takes is belief in yourself and hard work.

We hope they inspire you to follow your own dreams. Right now.

APPAREL AND FASHION

Brennan Agranoff, 13, HoopSwagg[35]/ PetParty[36]

Sherwood, Oregon, U.S.

Brennan Agranoff grew up in Oregon, not far from Nike's headquarters, and he and his friends *loved* Nike. But at age 13, when his pals started sporting the brand's $14 Elite basketball socks, Brennan wanted to stand out.

He bought a pair of brightly patterned socks online for $40 and spent nine months researching the printing process. He built a business plan, persuaded his parents to invest $3,000, and launched Hoop-Swagg—a playful brand that manufactures eye-catching basketball socks.

HoopSwagg stocks a mix of goofy designs: a melting ice cream cone, a spoof of the infamous Portland International Airport carpet, and a "goat farm" scattered with photos of the real animals on Brendan's family's property.

Five years later, he has twenty employees and 700 original patterns, and he's earning millions.

Putting off college to focus on the business, he recently launched a second company, PetParty, that prints on-demand socks featuring images of Fido and Cuddles.

"The concept of quick-turnaround, customized products is where I see the industry heading," he says.

Isabella Rose Taylor, 8, Isabella Rose Taylor[37]

Dallas, Texas, U.S.

Isabella Rose Taylor began painting at age 3 and designing jewelry at 8. She launched her fashion brand for young women at the same time and quickly landed in local retailers and boutiques.

A few years later she partnered with Nordstrom, and her designs spread across the country. But as sales rose into the high six figures, Isabella struggled with sourcing and manufacturing as she tried to scale on the fly.

"The Nordstrom deal forced us to handle growth very quickly," she says. "I was just putting out fires, when I really needed to scale back and restructure."

So, she did. She stopped working with large retailers and left her hometown of Austin to study fashion marketing at New York's Parsons School of Design; she's since moved home and is taking online business classes from New York University.

Isabella is now thinking strategically about partnerships, such as with Pottery Barn Teen, and has found partners to help her scale as she rebuilds her retail presence.

"I know more about manufacturing and distribution now, but I still don't have those years of expertise," she says. "With a strong team in place, I will have the luxury of thinking big-picture."

Moziah Bridges, 9, Mo's Bows[38]

Memphis, Tennessee, U.S.

Moziah Bridges started Mo's Bows in his grandmother's kitchen when he was 9 years old.

Moziah says it was his desire to find a sharp-looking fashion accessory that inspired him to launch his business.

In addition to bow ties, Moziah's Memphis-based company sells neckties, pocket squares, and men's accessories that are sold in various retail stores nationwide, including partnerships with Bloomingdale's and Neiman Marcus.

Moziah plans to study fashion design in college, and in the future hopes to own a large international clothing company that makes and sells clothes for men, women and children.

The best advice he ever received, he says, "came from my mentor Daymond John of Shark Tank. He told me to 'stay true to your brand.'

"That's important to remember, because there are a lot of different opportunities that come to me, but they may not be the best for me or the mission of my company."

As for his future, Bridges hopes to attend New York's Parsons School of Design and launch a full clothing line by age 20.

"I want to showcase all the skills I've learned," he says. But first things first, "I want to get my license and buy a Jeep."

BEAUTY AND BODY PRODUCTS

Daniel Schlessinger, 18, FixMySkin[39]

Omaha, Nebraska, U.S.

Eighteen-year-old Daniel noticed that his hands and lips were getting overly dry during the winter months. He tried all sorts of balms to no avail.

So, he decided to make his own.

Performing extensive research, talking to chemists and investing in over fifty different formulae, he eventually developed the perfect product.

It had to stand up to the cold winters in Nebraska and maintain its ability to spread easily, but also stay solid if placed in a warm pocket.

He calls it FixMySkin, and Daniel's product is hugely popular as a topical balm for dry skin. He earns over $60,000 in revenue every year.

Isabella Dymalovski, 14, Luv Ur Skin[40]

St. Kilda, Scotland, U.K.

Luv Ur Skin, an organization founded and managed by 14-year-old Isabella Dymalovski, is a natural skin-care line for girls developed with botanical ingredients. It includes body lotion, lip gloss, nail polish and moisturizers.

"I go into meetings and the people there all underestimate me and direct their questions at Mum instead of me," Isabella tells the *Herald Sun*[41].

"But then when I start answering the questions, they kind of sit up and realize that I'm actually the one in charge."

She believes the most important thing about the Luv Ur Skin line is she knows her target audience better than anyone.

"It's made for tweens, by a tween," she says. In the future, if she's not running her own successful business, "I'll be in a show on Broadway," she proclaims.

The best business advice that she strives to follow is, "Listen."

Kiowa Kavovit, 7, Boo Boo Goo[42]

Bronx, New York, U.S.

At 6 years old, Kiowa Kavovit confidently appeared on *Shark Tank* to pitch Boo Boo Goo, a natural, ecofriendly alternative to Band-Aids. The product gets painted onto the skin where the cut is, eliminating the need for bandages.

She was able to get a $100,000 investment, and production began, but Boo Boo Goo has since closed its doors as Kiowa has moved on to bigger ideas.

Her dad, Andrew, is also an inventor and says, "It's my hope that my children grow up thinking outside the box when it comes to careers; it will just give them more freedom in their lives later."

ENTERTAINMENT

David Dobrik, 17, David Dobrik's Vlogs[43]

Vernon Hills, Illinois, U.S.

In the early 2000s, MTV produced the series *Jackass*. Today, we have David Dobrik's vlogs.

David was born in Slovakia but moved to Vernon Hills, Illinois, at a young age, which is where he began producing internet content.

He first became a millionaire on the popular video app Vine, where he had over a million followers. He uploaded short comedy clips with his friends, and sponsors began to pay him for his work.

He then moved to Los Angeles and changed his comedic format over to YouTube, where he now writes, directs, films, and edits comedic skits, stunts and pranks.

Occasionally, he'll post a feel-good video with shock value, like surprising his friends with a free car. Each four-minute video contains several short, fast-moving, comedic clips.

His three-year-long relationship with Liza Koshy also opened his content up to another audience, and the two Viners-turned-YouTubers quickly rose to online stardom by 2017.

Though they ultimately split in 2018, Liza and David continue to make videos together as friends and remain in the same social circles.

David's unique style truly resonates with young people. Currently, he has over 18 million subscribers and his videos have 2.5 billion views.

His videos have become so popular that he has brought traditional celebrities into his vlog, like Josh Peck, Snoop Dogg, and Steve-O. According to SocialBlade, his content makes an estimated $9 million per year[44], and that doesn't take into account that he also gets paid for public appearances, his podcast, and sponsorships.

Gloson Teh, 12, Poet/Musician/App Developer[45]

Kuala Lumpur, Malaysia

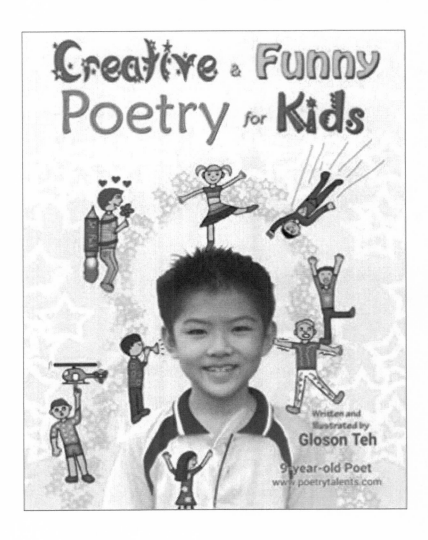

One of the few young entrepreneurs who's made it outside the world of technology, Gloson Teh is a published poet. At 12 years of age, his comedic poetry has been bought, read and adored by thousands of readers.

As well as traveling around Malaysia reading his poems, Gloson creates videos of him reading and acting out his poems, releasing several DVDs and creating a YouTube channel. Gloson even had the chance to meet the Prime Minister of Malaysia.

He also runs a blog where he gives tips on poetry; composes classical music (see one piece performed by the UiTM Orchestra here[46]); and develops apps such as Speed Mandarin, which helps people learn Mandarin "in a fun and easy way," he tells *The Guardian*[47].

Jeffrey Owen Hanson, 12, Painter[48]

Overland Park, Kansas, U.S.

While receiving chemotherapy for a condition affecting his nervous system, 12-year-old Jeffrey Owen Hanson discovered his talent in art.

Friends and family who came to visit him seemed overcome with sadness, so his mom got the idea to bring notecards for Jason to paint with watercolors for his visitors, to cheer them up.

Jeffery is also visually impaired by neurofibromatosis type 1—and so he began jokingly referring to his art as "a sight for sore eyes."

Over time, Jeffrey began to paint on canvases, and his artistic talent developed.

Thanks to the Make-A-Wish foundation, he met Elton John and handed him a painting. From there, he got many high-profile clients and began to rake in hundreds of thousands of dollars.

Now 26 and healthy, he still paints for a living, as well as running Jeffery Owen Hanson LLC, a philanthropic business benefiting children's cancer research.

Jojo Siwa, 11, Dancer, Singer, Actor[49]

Omaha, Nebraska, U.S.

Jojo Siwa was born in a small town in Nebraska and grew up learning how to dance at her mother's small studio since she was 2 years old.

Her parents could see her natural talent, and they pushed to get her in the spotlight. After appearing on two reality TV shows, *Abby's Ultimate Dance Competition* and *Dance Moms*, at age 11 Jojo began to establish an independent brand.

Jojo sells hair bows[50] and curates her own YouTube[51] channel, which has ten million followers; she also runs wildly successful TikTok and Instagram profiles.

She won the Kid's Choice Award for Best Social Media Star, and Nickelodeon gave her a TV show[52]. Her merchandise has appeared in Walmart, Target, Claire's, JCPenney, and other major retailers, and she is adored by kids and tweens worldwide. According to Celebrity Net Worth, she's currently worth at least $12 million.

Liza Koshy, 17, Comedian[53]

Houston, Texas, U.S.

Liza Koshy is a comedian, who uses her quick wit to make puns and create caricatures.

Liza started off on Vine with six-second videos and then moved on to creating her own YouTube channel, posting extended comedy videos, which became even more popular.

Also well-known on TikTok (still called *Musically* at the time), Liza had catapulted to internet fame by 2016.

Liza currently has over eighteen million subscribers, and a YouTube Original series called *Liza on Demand*.

Her personality caught the attention of traditional media, and she was invited to host the Met Gala in New York City and Nickelodeon's reboot of the *Double Dare* TV series.

She has received four Streamy Awards[54], four Teen Choice Awards[55], and a Nickelodeon Kids' Choice Award[56]. Liza also was included in the 2019 *Forbes*[57] 30 Under 30 Hollywood & Entertainment list and the *Time*[58] 2019 list of the 25 Most Influential People on the Internet.

According to Celebrity Net Worth, she's worth $6 million[59].

ENVIRONMENT

Greta Thunberg, 16, Environmental Activist/ Fridays for Future[60]

Stockholm, Sweden

Greta Thunberg is a 16-year-old climate activist responsible for the school strike in September 2019 that inspired millions of youth to take to the streets to advocate for the climate crisis.

She began her climate campaign when she was 15, by skipping school every Friday at her home in Sweden and standing outside Swedish Parliament holding a sign reading "School strike for climate" in Swedish.

Since then, she has spoken around the world, including at the United Nations Climate Change Conference, and was named *Time*'s 2019 Person of the Year.

She also takes personal actions in favor of the climate, such as not flying or eating meat.

Known for her unflinching ability to call out officials more than three times her age, and respected for her fervent commitment to her cause, Greta has moved politicians and officials worldwide to take further action.

Hannah Herbst, 17, Inventor[61]

Boca Raton, Florida, U.S.

In the summer of 2013, Hannah Herbst was the only girl at her summer engineering camp; but by the time that camp ended, she was on the winning team of the invention contest.

Hannah had discovered a passion for science and engineering that was furthered that year when she learned about energy poverty and the global water crisis.

Her 9-year-old pen pal from Sub-Saharan Africa explained to her that electricity was inaccessible for many people; this inspired Hannah to create a product that solved this problem.

Combining her newfound passion with a drive to change the world, Hannah created BEACON (Bringing Electricity Access to Countries through Ocean Energy), which brings reliable electricity and drinkable water to people who are unable to access them.

At age 15, she created an ocean energy probe prototype that seeks to offer a stable power source to developing countries using untapped energy from ocean currents.

Hannah has now spoken at numerous conferences and has been the recipient of multiple awards for her technology.

Jasilyn Charger, 18, Our Climate Voices[62]

Eagle Butte, South Dakota, U.S.

Jasilyn Charger is an indigenous rights and climate activist and a member of the Cheyenne River Sioux Tribe in Eagle Butte, South Dakota.

She writes that, in her childhood, she was focused on one powerful question: "How am I going to protect the land that our ancestors fought and gave their lives for, for us to utilize and prosper on?"

She is passionate about conserving the environment and the land that she and her ancestors have lived on for centuries. That led Jasilyn at age 18 to found the International Indigenous Youth Council during the Standing Rock Indigenous Uprising of 2016.

Now 23, she hopes to empower younger generations to become the spokespeople for their indigenous communities.

Jasilyn wants to continue her work for the rest of her life, saving both her community and her land.

Miranda Wang and Jeanny Yao, 22 and 21, BioCellection[63]

Vancouver, British Columbia, Canada

Miranda Wang and Jeanny Yao created their startup BioCellection in 2015 to solve the issue of plastics ending up in the ocean.

They invented a technology that repurposes formerly unrecyclable plastics into chemicals that are valuable to humans.

Each ton of plastic trash can be converted into over $2,500 of chemicals, and averts roughly twenty tons of carbon dioxide from being released into the earth.

"It's accurate to say," warns Miranda, "that plastic pollution is now a global crisis that doesn't just threaten the lives of millions of wildlife, but also is threatening the safety of literally everyone in this room and everyone on this planet."

Finance

Aaron Easaw, 18, Maatar Makers[64]

Fort Worth, Texas, U.S.

Maatar Makers (formerly ACE Venture Capital) is a VC firm created by Aaron Easaw, dedicated to investing and supporting entrepreneurs under 30. What makes his firm different is that it combines investments with relationships as a way to do due diligence and track progress of each startup.

Aaron believes that "age doesn't define your ability." He has developed several other corporations, including the multi-investor INC.UBATOR venture capital firm, which helps young businesses grow and gain the traction required to be successful.

Working hard to gain respect and recognition not only for himself but for teenage entrepreneurs around the world, Aaron has established himself as a bright mind of the future.

His motto: "Don't dwell on the past. Learn from your mistakes and move on." He speaks about his work here[65] on "20 Under 20," a podcast geared toward Gen Zers.

Erik Finman, 14, Bitcoin Investor[66]

Post Falls, Idaho, U.S.

When Erik Finman was 12 years old, he received $1,000 from his grandfather as a gift. Instead of buying video games and candy, he invested in Bitcoin, and held onto it.

He was not the best student at school; he earned only a 2.1 GPA. Most of his teachers thought he wasn't going anywhere in life. He told his parents how he hated school and wanted to drop out. Then, Erik struck a deal with his parents to skip college in pursuit of an unorthodox education, provided he could invest successfully and turn that $1,000 into $1 million by age 18.

He focused closely on cryptocurrency trading and made his first $100,000 selling Bitcoin when he was only 14.

By the time he was 19, the value of his Bitcoin had skyrocketed so high, he was a millionaire. At its peak in 2017, he had amassed a fortune in Bitcoin valued around $8 million.

His Instagram feed features ostentatious photos of himself stepping out of private jets or lying on beds covered in money, with captions like, "Cash so worthless compared to Bitcoin I'm sleeping on it …," says *The Guardian*[67].

Today, Erik has expanded his investment portfolio and uses his money to fund other entrepreneurial projects.

Vitalik Buterin, 19, "Initial Coin Offerings" for Bitcoin/Ethereum[68]

Toronto, Ontario, Canada

Vitalik Buterin was born in Russia, and his parents moved to Canada when he was 6 years old.

Right away, the school could see that Vitalik was a mathematical genius, and they put him in classes for gifted children. He later went to a private high school in Toronto.

He was interested in blockchain technology and was trying to figure out ways to improve it. He won $100,000 from the Thiel Fellowship after entering college, and began to write articles for *Bitcoin Magazine* on the side.

Receiving pay in the form of Bitcoin, which would not retain real significant value for another few years, Vitalik sought out ways he could improve the system.

In 2013, he co-created the white paper for the cryptocurrency platform Ethereum. This made it easy for new companies to create "Initial Coin Offerings" (or ICOs) for their own businesses, and millions of people around the world started to buy his cryptocurrency.

Since the value of Bitcoin and Ethereum fluctuate so quickly, it's hard to pinpoint Vitalik's true net worth, but at this point, he is valued at least for $500 million[69].

FOOD AND NUTRITION

Abby Kircher, 15, Abby's Better[70]

Baltimore, Maryland, U.S.

A homeschooled food lover and health enthusiast, Abby Kircher invented her first batch of healthy, good-for-you nut butters at age 15. Trying to stave her own rumbling appetite for a filling snack, she concocted five flavors.

What started as a hobby in her parents' kitchen soon became "Abby's Better," a brand distributed in the East Coast and Midwest through such chains as Wegmans and Lowes Foods, with annual revenue of over $1 million.

Abby currently manages twelve employees (including her parents and brothers) and has learned a lot about leadership.

"I've learned a lot of humility, that's for sure," Abby says. "You can't rely on just yourself or just your experience. You have to ask for help and advice and support."

Abby has given up a lot of valuable time to be a young CEO.

"There have been sacrifices in terms of not going out with friends or to parties because I'm making products or working on our marketing," she says.

"And I'm postponing college right now, which is a big sacrifice. But I regret nothing. Running a business is all-consuming in a way, but it's worth it because you know you're working toward your goals, not someone else's."

Cory Nieves, 6, Mr. Cory's Cookies[71]

Englewood, New Jersey, U.S.

When Cory Nieves was 6 years old, he dreamed of saving up for his own car, because he was tired of taking the bus to school. He'd need a *lot* of money for that.

First, he tried selling hot cocoa and lemonade, but then he began a quest to create the perfect chocolate chip cookie using all-natural ingredients.

After much trial and error, Cory and his mother, Lisa, perfected their recipe, and Mr. Cory's Cookies was born.

Through the cookie business, Cory has worked with Aetna, Citibank, Macy's, Whole Foods, Williams Sonoma, J. Crew, Viacom, and Pottery Barn.

Cory plans to continue to work as CEO of Mr. Cory's Cookies, "and grow the business into a multi-billion-dollar brand. I also want to be an angel investor, a chef and help people all around the world," he says.

His advice to other career-builders: "Stay humble, never give up, and always dream of six impossible things."

Haile Thomas, 12, Healthy Active Positive Purposeful Youth (HAPPY)[72]

Dallas, Texas, U.S.

Haile Thomas's venture, HAPPY, aims to improve the health and wellness of children by implementing programs that teach kids how to cook nutritious meals — many of which are free or affordable — and promote physical activity.

Haile began her journey when she was 12, working for Hyatt Hotels' "For Kids By Kids" menus.

Since then, she's spoken all over the world, joined on multiple occasions by former First Lady Michelle Obama, hoping to empower people to eat healthier.

She was inspired by her family's ability to reverse her dad's type-2 diabetes through conscious eating choices and an overall healthier lifestyle.

Now she's an international speaker, health activist, vegan food and lifestyle influencer, podcaster, and the youngest Certified Integrative Nutrition Health Coach in the United States.

Next, Haile would like to host "a televised plant-based cooking show showcasing vibrant, delicious and nutritious, plant-powered meals to the masses, to speak and share my message all around the world and continue to motivate youth to put their passion into action."

She's personally engaged over 35,000 kids with her activism and lives by this motto: "Be a leader, not a follower." You can check out her YouTube channel here[73].

Mikaila Ulmer, 15, Me and the Bees Lemonade[74]

Austin, Texas, U.S.

Mikaila Ulmer decided at age 4 to "make a difference in the world and save our [bee] pollinators" by opening a lemonade stand that raised funds for beekeeping.

Using a 1940s recipe from her grandmother for flaxseed-honey-sweetened lemonade, Mikaila directs a percentage of profits on her sales to "save the bees."

Having received $180,000 in funding from *Shark Tank*, Mikaila now sells through Whole Foods in a deal worth $11 million.

She says, "My biggest lesson about money is simple and has not changed since I was 4. Give, save, spend — in that order." She learned this from her dad.

She's been featured on Good Morning America[75], NBC News[76], and in Forbes[77] and Time[78] for her entrepreneurial success; has distribution deals with Wegmans and Whole Foods; and been invited to the White House — twice.

Claiming that she's done only what anyone would do, Mikaila has employed her entire family and gives talks on how bees pollinate crops, help flowers to grow and face diseases, and other global threats.

She says, "When I have a challenging day, if I know I saved a bee or inspired someone to be an entrepreneur, I know I am making a difference.

"I've been working hard not only to donate a portion of the proceeds [from lemonade sales] to help save the honeybees, but also speaking to Gen Z who have, in my opinion, a more social/activist mindset."

She says the best advice she's ever received was from her parents, who always encouraged her to dream big and that she could do anything she wanted. "I translated that into 'Beelieve,'" she says.

See videos about Mikaila's work at her YouTube channel[79].

Gaming and Sports

Kylian Mbappe, 16, Fútbol/Soccer[80]

Bondy, France

It's not surprising to hear of a young athlete becoming a millionaire, but it's particularly inspiring when someone is able to use their athletic abilities to improve their situation at a young age.

Kylian Mbappe[81] grew up in a poor suburban area outside of Paris, France. He played soccer nearly every day, and wished he could be like his idol, Cristiano Ronaldo. And it paid off.

Coaches took notice of his talent when he was just 6, and by 11 Kylian had his choice of teams to sign with.

He joined the AS Monaco Football Club with a $217 million contract when he was 16 years old and is the youngest person to ever sign with the team. He's also earned the second-highest signing bonus with his team.

Having been loaned out to multiple other French teams, as well as playing on France's 2018 World Cup winning team, Kylian is one of the youngest and most valuable players in the league, and his personal fortune is valued at an estimated $110 million.

Soleil "EwOk" Wheeler, 13, Fortnite Player[82]

Indianapolis, Indiana, U.S.

Soleil Wheeler, 13, is a deaf Fortnite livestreamer who goes by the name "EwOk."

She gained popularity when popular gamer Timothy John Betar ("TimTheTatman") once hosted her channel, thus giving her the attention of thousands of viewers.

EwOk's remarkable gaming ability becomes increasingly clear when you realize she must either communicate with other players through sign language on a webcam, or type in a second chat window, while simultaneously playing at an extremely high level.

Since joining the platform at age 13, EwOk has gained over 100,000 followers on Twitch, and competes regularly in Fortnite tournaments.

One of the youngest and the first female member of FaZe Clan, one of the world's top Esports organizations, EwOk is breaking down barriers within the gaming world for both girls and the deaf community.

Sumail Hassan Syed, 8, Esports Champion[83]

Karachi, Pakistan

Some parents try to discourage their kids from playing too many video games, but Sumail Hassan Syed discovered how to turn his hobby into a lucrative income.

Born in Karachi, Pakistan, Sumail started playing a game called Defense of the Ages ("DOTA") when he was 8 years old[84]. His parents did not have a lot of money, and they worked hard to move them to the United States, where eight people had to live together in a small apartment.

When he was 15, he had to sell his bicycle in order to keep playing the game.

This was a big deal for him, because his family did not have a car, and it was his only mode of transportation, but Sumail retained faith that his gaming career would one day find success.

Shortly after, he was able to join a team of professional video game players called "The Evil Geniuses."

Sumail specializes in DOTA 2, and his team is good enough to compete in tournaments that award monetary prizes.

In 2015, his team won the International DOTA 2 Championships in Seattle, Washington, and Sumail broke the Guinness World Record[85] for becoming the youngest esports player to become a millionaire, at 16.

After winning the prize money, he moved to Seattle and helped his family out financially. He still continues to compete in DOTA tournaments every year and earn more prize money.

Impact

Alex Wind, Cameron Kasky, Jaclyn Corin,
David Hogg, and Emma González, 17 to 19,
#NeverAgain[86]/Gun Control, Genocide, and
Human Rights Advocates

Parkland, Florida, U.S.

Beginning with the massacre at Columbine High School in Colorado, Gen Z has grown up preparing for and experiencing a growing number of school shootings in almost every state[87] in the U.S.

In the spring of 2018, David Hogg, Jaclyn Corin, Emma González, Cameron Kasky, and Alex Wind were at the center of a massive youth movement for gun control after surviving a massacre that killed seventeen of their classmates[88] at Marjory Stoneman Douglas High School in Parkland, Florida.

The five teenagers sparked the #NeverAgain movement, which saw thousands of students walk out of school[89] in a massive nationwide youth protest that swelled behind causes like stricter gun regulation and a general increase in youth participation in politics and policy.

They've continued their work as vocal advocates for advancing gun policies and youth participation through online campaigns, media appearances, and speaking tours[90].

What keeps them going? Cameron wrote in a Facebook post that he "Can't sleep. So angry ... I just want people to understand what happened and understand that doing nothing will lead to nothing."

Desmond Napoles, 12, Desmond Is Amazing[91]/"Drag Kid" and LGBTQIA Advocate

Manhattan, New York, U.S.

Desmond Napoles (stage name: Desmond is Amazing) is a 12-year old "drag kid," awarded LGBTQIA advocate, outspoken gay youth, editorial and runway model, public speaker, and founder of their own drag house (The Haus of Amazing). RuPaul, producer of wildly popular TV show *RuPaul's Drag Race*, dubbed Desmond "the future of America."

Desmond first developed an interest in drag when they were a toddler. Their mother would watch

RuPaul's Drag Race and they were stunned by the drag queens, with their flamboyant and decadent clothing and makeup.

Desmond made their professional drag debut in *RuPaul's Drag Race* Season 5 winner Jinkx Monsoon's video for the "Bacon Shake" when they were just 7 years old; since then, they've appeared on stages and runways across the world.

Desmond is an LGBTQIA advocate whose goal is to teach youth how to be themselves always and to pay haters no mind, because they "will never be as fierce as you and I."

Nominated for several awards, including the Qweerty Award, Shorty Award, and Social Global Impact Award, Desmond has been featured in Pride campaigns for Google and Converse.

They've appeared in *Vogue* magazine four times, breaking age and gender boundaries in the fashion industry.

Desmond has designed their own line of fans with Daftboy, T-shirts with Drag Queen Merch, and lashes with Chimera Lashes.

They recorded their first inspirational music single, "We Are All Amazing," in 2019, and the next year published a children's book called *Be Amazing: A History of Pride* for Macmillan Children's Publishing Group, to teach young children how to have self-confidence and express themselves.

They are currently working on a TV show and magazine for LGBTQIA youth, but looking to the future, they would like to study ornithology or engineering.

What inspires Desmond most is the feedback they receive from other youth who say Desmond has helped them discover the importance of self-expression and given them the courage to come out.

Desmond's motto is "Be Yourself, Always."

Isra Hirsi, 16, U.S. Youth Climate Strike[92]/ Activist

Minneapolis, Minnesota, U.S.

Daughter of Congresswoman Ilhan Omar, Isra grappled with harassment, safety threats, tokenization, and privilege on a national scale for years before she was even allowed to vote.

Isra founded the U.S. Youth Climate Strike — the American arm of a global youth climate change movement — alongside 12-year-old Denver activist Haven Coleman (who has since stepped away). As an environmental activist, Isra focuses on young people of color.

The organization has inspired 1.6 million students across 120 countries to skip school in order to demand action on climate change from adults in power.

Isra's advocacy has awarded her both positive and negative recognition, from inside her school's hallways to the pages of *Time* magazine and *Jacobin,* and the tweets of presidential candidates like Elizabeth Warren and Bernie Sanders.

The daughter of the first U.S. Somali-American legislator, and one of the first Muslim women (alongside Rashida Tlaib) to wear a hijab within Congress, Isra has activism in her blood.

"This puts Isra in a tricky position," notes *Vice*[93]. "She's both a symbol of supposed racial and religious equality in the U.S. — the kind that makes white women grin proudly at Black Muslim girls that aren't even her — and a teenager trying to figure out who she is in the wake of her mother's own colossal assertion of identity, all while staring down the serious task of literally saving the world."

Kelvin Doe, 11, Electrical Engineer[94]

Freetown, Sierra Leone, Africa

Born amid a civil war in Sierra Leone, then 6-year-old Kelvin Doe watched his community deal with a scarce electricity supply and consistent blackouts, and he set out to do something about it.

Beginning at age 11, he started collecting scraps of metal and discarded electronics in order to innovate a solution to providing electricity to nearby houses.

Just two years later, Kelvin had created a battery able to bring electricity to his and several surrounding homes, a radio transmitter, microphone receiver, sound amplifier, and three-channel mixer. After winning the top prize at a summer camp, he was invited to participate in a conference in Massachusetts and has since become an honorary board member of Emergency USA.

Presently, he runs the Kelvin Doe Foundation, a nonprofit organization seeking to empower African youth, and lives in Canada pursuing his education.

One day Kelvin hopes to run for President of Sierra Leone, where he will hopefully bring the same success he's seen personally to his country.

See his TED Talk here[95].

Malala Yousafzai, 15, Education Activist[96]

Mingora, Pakistan

Born in 1997, Malala attended her local school until age 11, when the extremist regime of the Taliban swept over her hometown of Mingora in the Swat Valley of Pakistan.

She continued to educate herself and, alongside her father, spoke out for girls' education.

In October 2012, on her way home from school, Malala was targeted and shot by members of the Taliban for her activism. She was moved to the United Kingdom for medical care, and from there was able to begin a new life and receive an education.

However, still determined to attain equal education rights for her home, she established the Malala Fund to help girls' education around the world.

She continues to speak out as an internationally recognized activist and the youngest-ever recipient of the Nobel Peace Prize. Malala is also a student at the University of Oxford.

You can read more on her incredible recovery and determination in her book *I Am Malala*[97].

Mihir Garimella, 17, Inventor of Flybrix Tiny Drone[98]

Pittsburgh, Pennsylvania, U.S.

A lover of robotics and "computer vision[99]," Mihir Garimella built Flybrix — a low-cost, intelligent drone for first-responders, that can enter and explore dangerous environments to find people who are trapped.

He completed this invention at age 14 and has spent the past four years developing and commercializing his product.

Currently an undergraduate at Stanford University, Mihir hopes in the future to "lead ambitious, high-impact research projects and bring them to the market.

"My future is still pretty open, and I'm not sure exactly what I'll work on, but I do know that I want to use computer science and robotics to make a difference."

Throughout his years at school, Mihir has already worked with Facebook, been involved with Google's self-driving car, and produced multiple apps.

What drives *him*? "Digging into problems that I see or experience."

Shamma bint Suhail Faris Mazrui, 22, Youth Advocacy

Abu Dhabi, United Arab Emirates

After obtaining her Bachelor's degree from New York University Abu Dhabi and becoming the United Arab Emirates' first Rhodes Scholar, Shamma earned her Master's in public policy from the University of Oxford.

She was then appointed Minister of State for Youth Affairs at age 22 — the youngest government minister in the world.

Landing a spot on the 2018 Forbes Middle East Arab 30 under 30[100] list, Shamma describes her role as a much larger effort to empower young people in the UAE to be active in their society and government.

"Arab youth are similar to youth all around the world," Shamma says.

She seeks to boost fellow young people's abilities. "We all want to go to the best universities, to have stable careers, and to have lives of purpose and feel a part of a cohesive community and family."

She has also worked in private equity, at the United Nations, and at the UAE Embassy in Washington, D.C.

INTERNET

Adam Hildreth, 14, Dubit Limited[101]/Crisp Thinking[102]

Leeds, West Yorkshire, England, U.K.

Adam Hildreth established his first company, Dubit Limited, an early social media platform, when he was 14. He and the seven friends with whom he launched his company made it into the *Guinness Book of Records*[103] for being the youngest group of directors in the U.K.

As Dubit became increasingly successful, Hildreth dropped out of high school to focus on growing the business.

By the time he was 19, the website had sponsorships with huge corporations like Coca-Cola, and he was worth $3.7 million. The social network became one of biggest teenage websites in the U.K. and later morphed into a "Youth Marketing Agency" that does research, strategy and digital development for child-centric marketing.

Adam could have stopped working at that point, but he wanted to do something truly great for the world. So, he developed Crisp Thinking, a cyber-protection company specializing in online child-protection technology for internet service providers (ISPs).

Crisp Thinking includes websites and games that are targeted at child audiences, and weeds out the language used by online predators and bullies who target young children on the internet. With a 98 percent success rate, his company has helped prevent countless numbers of children from becoming victims of predators.

Adam's net worth was projected to reach over $38 million in 2020.

Adam Horwitz, 15, Dirty Laundry/Mobile Monopoly[104]

Los Angeles, California, U.S.

When he was 15, Adam Horwitz made it a goal to become a millionaire by his 21st birthday.

After launching several startup websites, including his initial "Dirty Laundry" to share high-school gossip, Horwitz found success with Mobile Monopoly, which is an affiliate-marketing app that teaches users how to turn a profit with mobile market leads. He also started the text advertising service YepText.

In recent years, he has founded the "Wolves Talent" scouting site, based off using his personal experience to lead new creators to personal success, as well as launching a travel vlog YouTube channel.

Adam feels that the internet is the ultimate equalizer, because age does not determine one's success.

He says in a podcast with Incomediary[105], "I'm trying to help a lot of kids my age so they don't have to work at fast food places or [earn only] minimum wage.

"I want to show them that it is possible to make money online."

Carl Ocab, 13, Internet Marketing Services[106]/ Rich Kid Media

Manila, Philippines

First given internet access at age 12, Carl Ocab quickly picked up on the process of creating and developing websites. Within a year he had created carlocab.com, an internet marketing agency.

Quickly recognized due to his use of a high-result keyword, Ocab began growing his site, until it became one of the world's most widely recognized internet marketing agencies.

He has since discussed his success as a self-named "kidblogger" and hopes to encourage other young entrepreneurs to create and develop their ideas.

In this interview[107] he explains why the Philippines is a good outsourcing location to establish and grow your business.

He also runs Rich Kid Media, a web development and branding company.

Christian Owens, 14, Mac Bundle Box[108]/ Branchr Advertising

Corby, Northamptonshire, England, U.K.

After teaching himself how to code in middle school, Christian Owens started his first business at age 14 — and made his first million dollars in the next two years.

With Mac Bundle Box, Christian was able to offer simple, discounted Mac application packages after he negotiated with developers and manufacturers.

He used the power of group behavior to ensure sales: If a certain number of total people bought the Mac Bundle Box, a new application would be unlocked for all users.

He then founded Branchr Advertising, a pay-per-click advertising company that distributes 300 million ads per month on over 17,500 websites and smartphone applications.

The company, which aims to deliver "contextual, behavioral, and geographically targeted" ads on those platforms, made $800,000 in its first year and employs eight adults, including his mother, Alison.

Christian tells *Gizmodo*[109], "There is no magical formula to business. It takes hard work, determination, and the drive to do something great."

John Xie, 13, Cirtex[110]/Taskade[111]

Shanghai, China, and New York, New York, U.S.

At age 13, John Xie started an online web hosting service (receiving payments via PayPal) called Cirtex.

Today, the business has revenues of around $2 million and his clients range from those who are looking for the affordable to dedicated hosting servers.

After attending Babson College in Massachusetts, John has gone on to serve more than 300,000 clients and maintains a global staff in the U.S., Canada, India, and Brazil.

He has also launched Taskade, an online collaboration tool that helps teams get tasks accomplished, whether working in-person or remotely. As we progress through the COVID pandemic, sites like Taskade will be extremely necessary as they allow businesses to operate remotely.

Juliette Brindak, 16, MissOandFriends[112]

Greenwich, Connecticut, U.S.

Juliette Brindak is founder and owner of hugely famous website MissOandFriends.com, a place for young "tween" girls to interact with one another.

Girls can play games and ask for advice on the site, which provides a safe, secure and inviting place to build self-esteem. Subscribers can talk about their worries and dreams without stressing about being popular or fitting in.

Juliette is currently worth $15 million. Her revenue comes from online ads on her site, the "OMG Teen" book series that have sold over 120,000 copies, games, and toys.

View an early video[113] on how Juliette built her business from her girlhood sketches and imaginings.

Nick D'Aloisio, 17, Summly[114]/Sphere Knowledge[115]

Oxford, England, U.K.

Nick taught himself to code when he was 12 years old by developing apps for his iPod Touch, which he got as a present from his parents.

In school, he excelled in complex subjects like math and Chinese. At 15, he came up with an app called TrimIt, which improved the relevancy of search engine results.

While studying for GCSE mock exams, Nick realized that the search interface was antiquated: Looking up things and finding out information had to be done in roundabout methods that require too much time.

He decided to upload TrimIt to the Apple iTunes store, and it quickly got a lot of press coverage. A business magnate from Hong Kong, Li Ka-Shing[116], reached out to him and offered to put in $300,000 in funding for him to develop his app further.

Nick used that money to hire a team from Israel to help recalibrate the app into Summly, a mobile app which automatically summarizes news articles and other material.

Not only did the app help narrow down search results, but it would take an article and summarize the most important part of the story into a short paragraph that people could read on their phones, enabling them quickly to skim the news.

Six months later it was sold to Yahoo for $30 million. Yahoo turned it into their News Digest app, a modified two-times-daily digest of news based on the algorithms created by Nick when he started Summly.

Now a student at Oxford University, Nick will soon earn his doctorate in philosophy. Meanwhile, he's raised funds to develop a new app called Sphere Knowledge, that allows users to chat with experts in various fields.

Noa Mintz, 12, Nannies by Noa[117]

New York, New York, U.S.

Noa Mintz started her first business in 2008, running art classes for kids during the summer for a small fee.

Two years later, she founded a children's party planning business. To ensure her staff members were following workplace protocol, she wrote an employee handbook for them.

At 12, she discovered a gap in the market for an easy way to locate the best nannies available in any given area.

She used her firsthand experience of being a child in the city and founded Nannies by Noa, a full-service childcare agency that matches nannies with families and provides thorough background screening of and workshops for their nannies, as well as ongoing support for their users. The agency quickly earned Noa $375,000.

When she started high school and needed more time for schoolwork, Noa hired a fulltime CEO with twenty-five years of industry experience. She has since hired two additional associates.

"The best part by far is the fact that I am a job creator and have been able to get so many people employed," Noa says. "It is rewarding and empowering."

Noa says she's found nannies for hundreds of families in the New York area, and the primary referral source for her business is word of mouth.

The best advice she's ever received was from her middle school principal: "Early is on time, on time is late, and late is unacceptable."

Stephen Ou, 25, OhBoard and Other Ventures[118]

Kaiping, China

Stephen Ou launched five entrepreneurial projects before the age of 25. One of these is the OhBoard, a whiteboard application for the Google Chrome browser.

Now a software engineer at WhatsApp, he spearheads new feature development for the web client team and specializes in JavaScript — in particular, ES6, React, Node, Electron, and Flow.

Stephen says, "I have also dabbled a lot in Python, some in C++, and a little in Erlang."

While enrolled at Stanford University, he has conducted research projects in machine learning and natural language processing.

MARKETING

Farrhad Acidwalla, 16, Rockstah Media[119]

Mumbai, India

At 13, Farrhad Acidwalla borrowed $20 from his parents to create an online community based around aviation and plane models.

He quickly sold that platform and used the funds to create marketing agency Rockstah Media, an online business platform focused on web development and marketing.

By the time he was 17, Rockstah Media had become an internationally successful, award-winning agency, and Farrhad was a recognized TEDx speaker and the founder of multiple other businesses.

Now 25, Farrhad is a multimillionaire and investor, and hopes to make technology more accessible to the youth populations of India.

Jesse Kay, 17, 20 Under 20s[120] Podcast

Upper Saddle River, New Jersey, U.S.

In his junior year of high school, Jesse Kay created a podcast called "20 Under 20," in which he interviews successful entrepreneurs asking about practical tips they have for youth who are trying to get started in their endeavors.

Jesse firmly believes that Gen Z has the capacity to be just as, if not more, entrepreneurial than any previous generation.

As he describes it, growing up in a post-9/11 world and having experienced the pandemic and recession at an early age, Gen Z has learned firsthand that nothing is given in life.

In an age where as many as 85 percent of Americans "hate" their day job, Jesse hopes to teach future professionals that there are options outside of the 9-to-5.

Read more about his mission in *Thrive Global*[121].

Retail

Asia Newson, 5, Super Business Girl/Pretty Brown Girl[122]

Detroit, Michigan, U.S.

Known as Detroit's youngest entrepreneur, Asia Newson, now 14, makes and sells her handmade candles through her company, Super Business Girl.

She began selling candles door-to-door at age 5, and a few years later decided to spread her business model to lead other young entrepreneurs to success.

Now co-founder and CEO of Super Business Girl, Asia has been featured on *The Ellen DeGeneres Show* and *America's Got Talent,* and she was a keynote speaker for TEDx Detroit. Asia's mother and father serve respectively as president and director of sales for the company.

Ben Pasternak, 17, Several Startups, Currently Nuggs[123]

New York, New York, U.S.

Ben Pasternak started Flogg, a social community and virtual marketplace for teens to sell, buy and barter items within their own network. Saying he's committed to "changing the world and building the next Apple," he then went on to create Monkey, an app that connected people to random strangers. His latest venture is Nuggs[124], a nutritional startup selling "faux" meat products such as chicken nuggets and hot dogs. They piloted their products in the last few months of 2020 in grocery stores in California.

Ben calls his meat-alternative chicken "the Tesla of meat."

The best advice he's ever received: "One of my mentors Chris Smith told me to drop out of high school and move to NYC. I did and have no regrets."

Benjamin "Kickz" Kapelushnik, 16, Sneakerdon.com[125]

Ft. Lauderdale, Florida, U.S.

At only 16, Benjamin "Kickz" Kapelushnik created a rare trainer reselling website as a hobby.

As his business grew, he began to gain celebrity clients including DJ Khaled and Odell Beckham, alongside an ever-growing customer list.

As he made more contacts, Benjamin was able to bulk buy sought-after items. His sales are now worth over $1 million. Read an in-depth feature on him here[126].

"The best advice was from my mom," he says. "Follow your dream and your passion."

Maddie Bradshaw, 10, M3 Girl Designs[127]

Dallas, Texas, U.S.

When she was 10, Maddie Bradshaw wanted to decorate her locker. Since there wasn't anything on the market that interested her, she started to decorate soda bottle caps.

Maddie then became the founder and president of M3 Girl Designs, hired her mother and sister, survived *Shark Tank*, and authored a book titled *Maddie Bradshaw's You Can Start a Business, Too!*[128], to inspire other young entrepreneurs.

She made her first million by age 13, and at 16, she was selling over 60,000 of her unique bottle cap necklaces a month and making over $1.6 million annually.

Maddie tells *Digital Journal*[129], "The great thing about our company is that it's growing with me. As my tastes change, so will the products."

Her advice to other young entrepreneurs is to "follow your passion. If you come up with an idea and you love it, chances are other people will, too."

Since then, she's closed up the company to focus on college at Stanford.

Nic Bianchi, 12, Bianchi Candle Co.[130]

Grandola, Italy

Now 16 years old, Nic Bianchi started Bianchi Candle Co. when he was 12. He says he put his love of math and science to work to design wonderful smelling, all-natural, handmade candles.

Each batch of Bianchi's candles is hand-poured in small batches and made of all-natural soy wax that burns longer and cleaner. The candles are designed in Italy and produced in Nebraska.

Rachel Zietz, 13, Gladiator Lacrosse[131]

Boca Raton, Florida, U.S.

Rachel Zietz's company, Gladiator Lacrosse, sells lacrosse equipment, including backyard goals and rebounders.

Rachel says her company, which is on target to exceed $2 million in revenue this year, recently acquired All Ball Pro with the intent to expand into other sports. Her gear also was used at the World Lacrosse Championship, which was broadcast on ESPN.

"The school day is the same as the business day," she tells *Entrepreneur*[132] magazine. "So, it's a lot of time management and explaining to teachers that you have to miss part of the day because you're speaking at a conference about your business."

Now at Princeton University studying economics, she plans to continue building her business.

She envisions a career "doing something business-related," Rachel says. "I don't know what the future will hold for me, but I hope that I can look back and say that I somehow left my mark in the sport of lacrosse." She tries to bring fierce determination to everything she does.

Sean Belnick, 14, BizChair[133]

Canton, Georgia, U.S.

As a young teenager in middle school, Sean Belnick started selling online with small items like Pokémon cards on eBay. He started BizChairs when he was 14 years old — long before Amazon and other sites offered online purchasing with free delivery.

BizChairs, an online office furniture website, offers simple designs as well as ergonomic and very trendy options. The drop-ship company removes the middleman and allows consumers to order online without visiting stores.

This simple idea was started with only a $500 loan (for advertising costs, from his stepfather) and around 100 products. He shares with Retire@21[134] the story of how he locked himself in his bedroom for three days and emerged with his company.

Soon, his customers included Abercrombie and Fitch, Microsoft and Google. By the time he turned 20, his business had already brought in $24 million in revenue.

Today, Sean has a warehouse in excess of 300,000 square feet and his clients include Google, the Pentagon and Microsoft. He's worth an estimated $42 million.

SOCIAL AND RACIAL JUSTICE

Akil Riley and Xavier Brown, Both 19, Black Lives Matter Protestor Activists[135]

Oakland, California, U.S.

Akil Riley and his best friend Xavier Brown felt compelled to organize the Oakland Tech High School March in Oakland, California, following the video that surfaced of George's Floyd's murder by the Minneapolis police.

On June 1, 2020, Akil and his friends rallied[136] with 15,000 other individuals to march across Oakland in support of Black Lives Matter. They wound up at the historic Oscar Grant Plaza. Although the protestors were peaceful, they were met with violence by the police.

Akil attributes much of his knowledge to doing his homework, reading works by great writers, and educating himself to know his history.

Since his June 1st march, Riley has co-organized another protest for the death of Erik Salgadoa as well as a Juneteenth event with a youth group, BY4PL. Akil and Xavier inspire us to use our voices, no matter how young we are, to create change and to stand up for what we believe in.

Amika George, 20, Free Periods[137]

London, England, U.K.

Amika George became aware of the stigma around menstruation after reading an article about how many British women miss school because they are unable to afford sanitary products to protect them during their periods. So, at age 17, she founded Free Periods.

Her company seeks an end to "period poverty," as well as pushing for increased access to education for girls.

A year after Amika began the Free Period campaign, which sought the provision of free menstrual products to all students within the national free-lunch program, she saw triumphant results: The British government made period products free in British schools.

Amika continues to fight for equal access to education, as well as pushing increased menstrual education for both boys and girls.

She is currently attending Cambridge University, and hopes to one day destigmatize periods in both the U.K. and around the world.

Brea Baker, 25, Justice League NYC[138]

New York, New York, U.S.

Brea Baker is a recent Yale University grad and founder of the Head 2 Toe Foundation, a nonprofit organization that works to support women and girls around the globe.

While at Yale, Brea acted as president of the campus chapter of the NAACP during a nationally scrutinized email scandal, which sparked a conversation about free speech, community and safety for people of color on college campuses.

She often participates in campaigns, from Women's Marches to gun violence walkouts to the #FreeMeekMill campaign.

Brea also works for Justice League NYC, as co-chair for the Board of Activists for COMMUNITYx, and as Grassroots & Community Liaison for Justice for Black Girls.

Presently an executive assistant at The Gathering for Justice, Brea continues to work for social change and global equality.

Hadiqa Bashir, 13, Girls United for Human Rights[139]

Swat Valley, Pakistan

Hadiqa Bashir follows in the footsteps of the strong women to come out of the Swat Valley, working to change the practices and perspectives around child marriage.

At just 11 years old, Hadiqa learned that her grandmother wanted to marry her off in accordance with local customs. But with the help of her progressive uncle Erfaan Hussein, she was able to push off the marriage.

Shortly after her personal experience avoiding her own forced child marriage, Bashir worked with her uncle to found Girls United for Human Rights.

As a student, she would often travel to houses and educate women about why child marriage was wrong. Hadiqa has successfully cancelled five child marriages in her community and helped domestic abuse survivors through her organization.

She currently attends school at Government Girls Higher Secondary School Saidu Sharif, as well as acting as chairperson at Girls United for Human Rights Foundation.

Now 18, she hopes to continue her fight for gender equality on a global scale.

Joshua Wong, 23, Scholarism[140]

Hong Kong, China

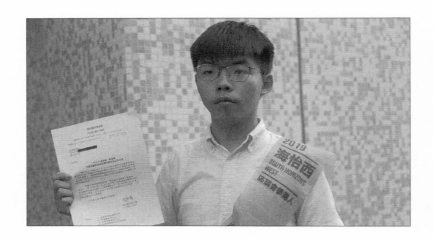

Joshua Wong is a student activist fighting for democracy and a change in the electoral system in Hong Kong.

He attended his first protest when he was 13, participating in the 2010 anti-high-speed rail protests.

Soon after, Joshua and a schoolmate founded Scholarism, a small student activist group initially working with basic protesting, but that soon grew into a large coalition of over 100,000 in attendance at rallies.

In June 2014, Scholarism spearheaded a plan to change the electoral system in Hong Kong for a more democratic, "one country, two systems" organization.

Joshua was pivotal in his involvement with the Umbrella Movement, marked by protesters using umbrellas to protect themselves from the use of pepper spray, which came out of the 2014 protests. He was arrested in September during a pro-democracy protest with 77 other people.

Joshua continues his efforts towards a democratic system in Hong Kong today.

Nupol Kiazolu, 18, Youth Coalition for Black Lives Matter of Greater New York/ Vote2000[141]

Brooklyn, New York, U.S.

When she was 13 years old, Nupol Kiazolu wore a black hoodie to school with the phrase "Do I look suspicious?" painted on the back.

She protested quickly after the murder of Trayvon Martin, noting that this type of violence was personal to her, as she had herself lost family and friends to police brutality.

Nupol has served as the President of the Youth Coalition for Black Lives Matter of Greater New York and attended countless protests across the nation to stand up for racial justice.

She began a new campaign titled Vote2000 to encourage youth of color to make their voices heard in elections, and she is continuing that work through this election cycle.

Watch out, because her dream is to be elected President of the United States in 2036!

Thandiwe Abdullah, 16, Black Lives Matter Youth Vanguard[142], Black Lives Matter in School Program[143]

Los Angeles, California, U.S.

Thandiwe Abdullah is a 16-year-old from the Crenshaw District in Los Angeles. She was just 10 years old when Black Lives Matter was founded, but she felt strong ties to the cause and a passion to change her community through the movement.

Now, Thandiwe is the co-founder of Black Lives Matter Youth Vanguard and was essential in creating the Black Lives Matter in School Program, which was nationally adopted. She has participated in countless protests, written letters, showed up at offices, and been successful in ending random searches in the Los Angeles Unified School District.

During the summer of 2020, Thandiwe was extremely active in the organization and leading of BLM marches in New York City as President of Black Lives Matter Greater New York. She plans to continue to lead the fight against racial injustice as she earns her BA at Hampton University.

Her biggest goal in life is to erase the idea of individual success. She says, "I'd want to see a culture shift, getting rid of the idea that in order to make it anywhere and be successful, you're on your own. I want everyone to care about other people. I want people to think that their own success and justice is tied to everyone around them. That's my world."

Ziad Ahmed, 21, JUV Consulting[144]

Princeton, New Jersey, U.S.

Being placed on a TSA watchlist as a child enabled Ziad Ahmed to see societal and racial injustice in his community based on factors people could not choose.

He created Redefy, an online platform dedicated to highlighting the differences between cultures, celebrating them, and defying the stereotypes.

He later launched JUV Consulting, a Gen Z marketing consultancy, for which Ziad serves as CEO.

The JUV team consists only of employees born after 1996, yet works with companies such as VSCO and Unilever to change the way companies promote to Generation Z.

Ziad has given several TEDx Talks and was named in Forbes' 2019 *30 Under 30* issue at age 19. Ziad is working to give young people a seat at the table, every time and all the time.

SOCIAL MEDIA

EvanTube, 8, EvanTube[145]

Pennsylvania, U.S.

With the assistance of his dad, Evan was 8 years old when he started his own YouTube channel, simply titled EvanTube[146], which reviews toys and discusses things that kids are into.

He also runs two additional accounts, EvanTubeRAW and EvanTubeGaming, which have allowed him to reach an audience far larger than that of just his toy reviews.

Now 13 years old, Evan's work on YouTube has become a family affair, as his sister Jillian, as well as his parents, have made appearances.

The channel brings in about $1.3 million annually.

Evan Spiegel and Bobby Murphy, 21 and 23, Snapchat[147]

Palo Alto, California, U.S.

Evan and Bobby met at Stanford University, where they developed an app based on the idea of disappearing photos, allowing users to feel freer with the ways they were sharing moments and photos with their friends.

They called the first edition of their app "Picaboo" but would eventually change the name to Snapchat.

Early on in their development, Facebook offered them $3 billion to purchase their idea, but the co-founders turned it down. Instead, they released their app in 2011. Evan was 23 and Bobby 25 when they would begin their rise to eventual billionaires.

The app now has over 210 million daily users and continues to grow as one of the world's most popular social media platforms for users under 30. The co-founders now own collectively around a third of the company and are worth $5.1 billion and 4.9 billion respectively.

Kristopher Tate, 20, Zoomr, EVER/IP[148], connectFree k.k.[149]

Tokyo, Japan

Kristopher Tate, ahead of his time in seeing the value of open-source photography, invented one of the most successful websites on the internet: Zoomr, which allowed people to upload pictures, edit them, and tag them to each other.

Kristopher says, "I'm just some guy with a camera. I try to take at least one photo every day."

That website was highly social and is praised for its accuracy, speed, and effectiveness in connecting people. Kristopher has now morphed his work into open-source coding and an app that connects you with stocked goods inside your favorite stores: EVER/IP and connectFree k.k.

Loren Gray, 12, Musician[150]

Pottstown, Pennsylvania, U.S.

One of the most followed celebrities on the TikTok platform, Loren Gray Beech had a large following on musical.ly (the former name of TikTok) by sixth grade — and because of the attention she received online, she began to experience severe bullying from her classmates.

Moving to Los Angeles, she quit school and built up a huge fan base with her singing and blogging. Loren was nominated for "Choice Muser" at the 2016 and 2018 Teen Choice Awards[151], and "Muser of the Year" at 2017 Shorty Awards[152].

Since then, Loren has signed with Virgin Records, released several bestselling singles, and maintains six Instagram accounts.

She has 47 million TikTok followers, making her the second most followed creator on the app, and her YouTube channel brings in $176,000 annually, according to statsmash.com.

Ryan Kaji, 2, Ryan Toys Review[153]/Ryan's World[154]

Houston, Texas, U.S.

The newest generation of small children are known to be glued to their iPads, but have you ever wondered what they might be watching?

It turns out some of those kids are mesmerized with watching toy unboxings and reviews.

Two parents who knew how to capitalize on their adorable son's excitement about opening a new toy started a YouTube channel called "Ryan Toys Review" when Ryan was just 2 years old.

Today, they have over 21 million subscribers who view their daily videos; their channel is in the top 100 in the U.S. and their videos have received over 30 billion views.

According to the YouTube revenue tracking website SocialBlade[155], the ad revenue from those videos makes anywhere from $2 million to $32 million per year. That doesn't take into account the fact that YouTubers get paid thousands of dollars by companies to advertise their products, plus they get free toys as well.

After the videos are complete, Ryan's parents donate many of the toys to charity.

The Verge[156] describes Ryan's World as "a mashup of personal vlog and 'unboxing' video, a blend of innocent childhood antics and relentless, often overwhelming consumerism." According to *Forbes*[157], Ryan was the highest-paid YouTuber in 2018, earning $22 million from his videos and product line at Walmart.

His work is not without controversy, however. A complaint filed in 2019 by Truth in Advertising[158] and the Federal Trade Commission claimed that they did not properly disclose sponsored content, and that "nearly 90 percent of the Ryan Toys Review videos have included at least one paid product recommendation aimed at preschoolers, a group too young to distinguish between a commercial and a review."

STEM AND TECHNOLOGY

Jason Li, 15, iReTron[159]

Los Gatos, California, U.S.

Beginning his freshman year of high school, Jason Li liked to fix iPhone and iPod screens as a way to make extra cash. However, he grew increasingly unsatisfied with the way electronics were thrown out; so, he invented a better solution for recycling them.

At age 15, Jason became the founder and proprietor of iReTron, an electronics refurbishment company.

With a $2,000 loan from his father, Jason created the company from his bedroom. The company buys old electronics from people, refurbishes them and sells them for a profit. Then in 2014, *Shark Tank* reached out to ask if he'd like to appear on their show, and Jason walked away with a $100,000 investment.

Still CEO of iReTron, he has created two other startups while in college. When asked what advice he has for budding entrepreneurs like him, Jason said they should never give up.

Omar Raiyan Azlan, 11, Mathematician/ Soccer Player

Abu Dhabi, United Arab Emirates

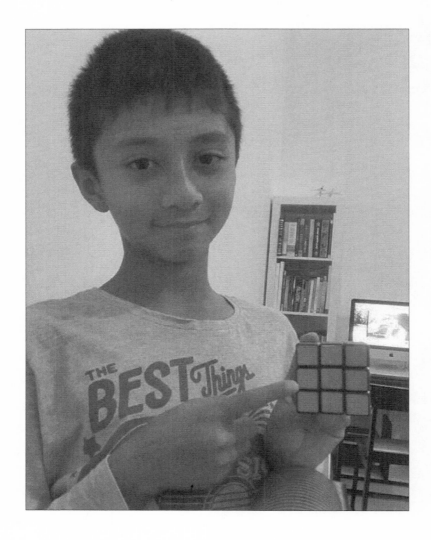

Some Gen Zers are just getting started, and one such example is the extremely talented Omar Azlan. Omar has won many Math Olympiads since his primary school days. He has beaten contestants from Asia, Europe, and America; and he's able to solve the Rubik's Cube in forty seconds.

He also plays fútbol (soccer). He joined the Manchester City junior team in the U.K. at age 9, winning Player of The Season once and Player of The Term three times.

Other interests include playing piano and speaking four languages — Malay, English, French, and Arabic. Now 14, Omar continues to excel in school and at sports, and has a bright future ahead of him.

Shubham Banerjee, 12, Braigo Labs[160]

Hasselt, Belgium

Founded by Shubham Banerjee when he was 12 years old, Braigo Labs creates Braille printers to help the visually impaired access expensive technology.

Shubham's invention uses LEGOs and robotics to design a product and sell it at less than half the price of others on the market.

His latest model uses Wi-Fi and Bluetooth to automatically print text from a website and translate it into Braille.

He's the youngest entrepreneur ever to receive venture capital funding. Banerjee envisions his future career "in a field that merges technology and medicine. Surgical procedures with robotics or human health would be great for me."

The best advice he ever received was to "be humble" and "innovate for the right reasons — money is not one of them."

TRANSPORTATION

Caleb Nelson, 16, Romeo's Rickshaws[161]

Cedar City, Utah, U.S.

Caleb Nelson, age sixteen, who lives in Cedar City, Utah, opened Romeo's Rickshaws[162] with his dad in 2017. They advertise not only a ride, but a local guide to the city as well.

The pedicab business started during the Utah Shakespeare Festival, one of the biggest tourist events in Cedar City and the state. Caleb initially came up with the idea after listening to his father, a real estate mogul, discuss how to draw more residents to the area.

Caleb doesn't actually charge for rides, though he accepts tips. Romeo's Rickshaws are also available for weddings and other events.

George Matus, 18, Teal[163]

Salt Lake City, Utah, U.S.

When George Matus was 17 years old, his fascination with aviation and drones inspired him to launch his own company, Teal.

The company sells commercial drones, some of which are presently the fastest on the market. Its first product was a battery-operated, camera-equipped unmanned aerial vehicle that reached speeds of 70 mph. The company seeks to make drones more accessible to the public and improve their design.

George has raised $2.8 million in seed funding and is a Thiel Fellow[164]. View this video[165] on how he invented his first drone. His company now employs thirty people and has raised $16 million in venture funding.

He credits his success to believing that one's dreams can come true, as well as having a big backyard and parents who "kept telling me to find what I love."

Ray Land, 17, Fabulous Coach Lines[166]

Branford, Florida, U.S.

Can a charter bus service make millions? Yes, it can. Ray Land wanted to be a truck driver from the time he was a little kid. By high school, he'd grown to hate the school buses chartered for away games and other events: dirty, bumpy, uncomfortable, and either no or filthy restrooms.

So at 17, he bought "an old rust bucket," he tells *Inc.*, and refurbished it with his own money. After graduating from high school, Ray — who had gotten his commercial driver's license and was driving one of the coaches himself — tried attending North Florida Community College for a while. It didn't stick. "All the papers I tried to write turned into brochures for my business," he says.

Today, Fabulous Coach Lines has over 200 employees and its buses offer red carpet entryways, espresso machines, and even seat-back monitors. One of Ray's 56-passenger buses rents for just over $1,000 per day; they've even transported the White House Press staff.

When Hurricane Katrina hit, Ray secured a contract to move displaced survivors; the U.S. military hired him and revenues in 2010 were around $4.3 million.

However, owning your own business comes with as much potential for tragedy as triumph. The next year, a university student involved in a hazing activity aboard one of Land's buses died, and the family sued Fabulous Coach Lines.

Later, he also co-founded a mobile app software company, and is now building a mega rest stop off an abandoned exit off Interstate 75 in Florida.

Moving to California in 2014, he launched Dreamtech, a company that buys double-decker buses and converts them into luxury tour buses. According to *The Gainesville Sun*[167], he manages five startups and is always pushing himself to do more. "If a person can dream it, we can build it," he says.

You can meet Ray and view a brief video on his company in this article[168] by *Inc.*

TRAVEL AND REAL ESTATE

Alex Hodara, 21, Hodara Real Estate Group[169]

Boston, Massachusetts and Jersey City, New Jersey, U.S.

Alex Hodara started his first year at Boston University riding around in taxicabs, checking out rental listings that he would then connect with other students. He spent $2,000 on cab fare, he reports to B.U.'s Questrom School of Business[170]. But by the time he graduated, he'd made his first million.

His company, Hodara Real Estate — now called Colivo — opened in 2009 and since then has acquired more than seventy properties and sold more than $5 million in investment type properties[171] with the help of fellow college students as employees. He quickly discovered that students trusted him and his peers more than older real estate agents.

Alex takes a comfort-first approach to building his career. "I'm not a big fan of going outside my comfort levels, so throughout my career I've always calculated the downside," he says.

"Figure out what it is you can lose — time, money, sleep — and then get focused. You know your downside and you're OK with it, so strive for that upside," he advises.

And just when he graduated college and put together a seven-building deal that would have netted a fortune, Alex started celebrating too soon; the deal imploded the day before closing. He says he learned to be more accountable to himself and never take his eye off the end goal.

Today, his company offers property management services, virtual tours and a reality TV show about their operations, "Making Moves[172]."

Tapping into the shared economy approach preferred by many Millennials and Gen Zers, Alex has now transitioned to Colivo[173], an experimental co-living company in which potential tenants, called members, sign up for around $1,000 per month (all inclusive) and are matched with roommates in fully furnished, multi-bedroom apartments that include gym memberships, weekly house cleaning, Netflix memberships, PlayStation 4 gaming systems, and regular Colivo-sponsored social events.

Alex made *Businessweek*'s "Top 25 Entrepreneurs Under 25" and *Forbes'* "30 Under 30"[174] lists and is reputed as having closed over $1 billion in real estate deals.

Bella Tipping, 12, Kidzcationz.com[175]

Dubbo, New South Wales, Australia

Bella Tipping had a really bad experience at a hotel where she didn't feel welcome as a kid, so she wanted to make vacations more fun for kids. "I want to change the way kids travel," she told *Fortune*[176].

"I want restaurant owners to look beyond the chicken nuggets and chips on the kids' menu and to make sure their venue is fun for all ages."

At age 12, she crafted a business plan and pitched it to her parents. She convinced them to invest $80,000 into Kidzcationz, a travel review website (similar to Expedia or TripAdvisor) that enables kids to rate hotels, restaurants, and attractions, based on how well they support their needs — especially families with special-needs kids.

"I didn't even know what an entrepreneur was," Bella tells Kebloom.com[177]. "I just considered myself a kid who wanted to help other kids and learn about business along the way." She says developing a thick skin has been critical to her survival, and that now when she hears the word "no," she simply views that as a chance to stop, listen, and go back to the drawing board and re-envision her goal.

So far, the site runs only in Australia, New Zealand, and the U.S., but Bella says she hopes to expand.

Kidzcationz focuses on what kids need — such as comfy beds, kid-friendly food, and parks and attractions. It keeps young users safe by allowing them to use avatars; they don't upload pictures or reveal any personal information.

Next, Bella plans to write a funny book and gaming app about her dog Jed. She sees her long-term career as one of "fighting for social change, because I want to live in a world where everyone is included."

Bella firmly believes for herself and all Gen Zers that "if you can think it, you can do it."

Like many Gen Zers, Bella wants to dedicate her career to making the world a better place. She tells MillennialEntrepreneurs.com, "My goal is to fight for social change. I want to live in a world where everyone is included."

Chapter 4: Achieving YOUR Dream: How-Tos and Further Resources

Ready to get from dream to done?

Browse this chapter for succinct tips and best practices for applying for internships and jobs, preparing for interviews, composing resumes and LinkedIn profiles, communicating courteously and professionally, negotiating salary, and more.

Job-Hunting During the COVID Pandemic

Impact of COVID on Gen Z

The oldest members of Gen Z have been hit hardest by COVID-19, a novel coronavirus discovered in 2019 that shut down countries around the world in 2020.

Gen Zers, having just graduated high school or college, or halfway through school but suddenly limited to online learning, experienced a double whammy:

1. More than any other age group, Gen Zers worked in service industries such as retail, transportation, food, and hospitality—and lost their jobs during shelter-in-place ordinances.

And it remains to be seen whether these jobs will come back, in some altered form or at all.

2. If you didn't have job experience yet, how would you get it now?

One-third[178] of Gen Zers lost their jobs during the pandemic, according to Pew Research, and that's higher than any other age group. One-third have experienced cancelled interviews, almost 30 percent have had their hours cut, and overall Gen Zers took an average pay cut of $6,000 in 2020, according to a study by Collegefinance.com[179].

Younger job candidates lack experience or are in entry-level positions that make their jobs the most vulnerable of all.

Double-Whammy: Pandemic + Recession

What makes things even more difficult is trying to enter the workforce during a depressed economy. Even before the pandemic hit, Gen Z's unemployment rate was higher than other groups: According to Pew, when the overall unemployment rate hovered around 10 percent in 2020, the level for those ages 16 to 24 was 28.4%[180].

"For Gen Z," says *The Guardian[181]*, "life has practically been upended and the ramifications of the virus and the financial crisis it has engendered threatens their livelihoods for years to come."

If you feel like the odds are stacked against you before you even apply for a job, hold on; we've got your back. This section will give you helpful tips to get you on your way to employment, in ways you might not have considered.

And remember, you're a **Gen Zer** — it's in your generational DNA to take matters into your own hands to change your world for the better.

Virtual Internships

Many employers have adapted both jobs and internships into virtual work[182], according to Handshake[183], an online career resource for college students.

"We're seeing a lot of employers really embrace the notion of the virtual internship, and they're trying to make the most of that by figuring out how to ensure students are still going to get the same learning," says Christine Cruzvergara. "They are still going to be able to build those relationships and make a good impression and impact on the company, and have a good time while they're in that experience as well."

A remote internship can allow you to build skills and beef up your resume ... even if you're prone on your bed in your pajamas while doing so.

Communicate, Communicate, and Check in Again

Even if you pride yourself on being a good communicator, buckle up, because you're in for a wild ride when it comes to remote-work relations.

Videoconferencing can help, but during most of your work hours, you don't have the benefit of observing your supervisor's body language and workaday habits.

We two writers, for example (Sanam and Suzanne), have relied on weekly telephone check-ins, every one of which starts with, "How are you doing during this weird [pandemic] time?" and ends with, "Is there anything else concerning you/on your mind?"

We've talked about various aspects of life, such as the weather outside our respective windows, and the eccentricities of our family members in quarantine, that may seem off-topic — but actually do wonders to help us build mutual trust and improve our ability to work as a team.

You cannot ask too often, "How's it going for you?" Ask direct questions about whether you're on track with your productivity and quality of work.

Autonomy Rules

All the power you feel you've lost in the economy, society, and immunity, has now flipped over and put you into full control of yourself and your time.

If you're an introvert, brew your cup of coffee and hunker down to work. If you're an extrovert, get a job as an online chat agent, take breaks to video chat with friends, talk your family's ears off in the kitchen, or better yet, call a lonely grandparent who can't get enough of your news.

You might try mapping out your day, scheduling regular wakeup times (bonus: you'll sleep better), adding more fitness and mindfulness, work periods and breaks. More than ever before, you rule.

Schmooze with Your School

No one sympathizes more with your situation than your teachers, professors, administrators, and career/

guidance counselors. Be cheerful and courteous but barrage them with requests for referrals — whether for an internship with the dean's spouse's company or a job doing lesson-planning research for your favorite teacher.

If the position you seek lies beyond your school's networks, at least ask people in your academic community for references. Always make sure to check with that person before you give out their name as a reference: Not only is this best practice; it's also a keen way to get them thinking about your skills in advance of being queried.

Acquire a New Skill

Ask yourself: Where do my dream job and the changing job market intersect? Maybe you have talent hidden inside one of your hobbies.

For example, our MY JOB intern, 18-year-old Sarah Helly, felt that COVID kidnapped the second half of her high-school senior year, prom, and graduation. Instead of starting college the next fall, she opted for a gap year.

Sarah never could have predicted what happened next.

She loves to create textile- and tattoo-style art and, in a simple desire to reach out beyond her quarantine bedroom, she posted several of her graphics on TikTok ... and watched in shock as her post received over 200,000 shares, and so many requests to purchase her artwork that she launched a new business on Etsy.

Or, maybe it's time to sate your curiosity about a job you secretly covet. As nearly all learning shifts to onscreen, it's more affordable and practical than ever to get ready for your career online. You already know you can learn anything from YouTube. Gen Zers are pros at finding answers and teaching yourselves. So, take advantage!

Coursera[184] offers 3,800 courses in computer science, data science, job skills, and career search courses. EdX[185] provides access to over 2,500 courses from universities all over the world. Khan Academy[186], whose free tutoring you may already have accessed, has added curricula materials to support learning on your own during COVID. And if you're not sure where to start with online learning, try Class Central[187], an online "matchmaker" between the field you desire and what courses you need to get you there.

You may have to pay to earn a certificate in your new field. However, if you've been laid off from your job, you may be able to earn course certificates for free[188] on Coursera.

Advice from a Millennial: Keep in Touch

It's about whom you know, Evergreen College graduate (and Millennial) Megan Jeffrey tells the *Seattle Times[189]*, so cultivate all of your relationships.

"Never take anyone in your life for granted, because you'll never know how they will impact your life. Never burn bridges you don't have to, because during the recession when I graduated, and even more so now, finding a job is really about who you know, and who knows you ...

"If you can cultivate your network and keep in touch with as many people as possible, that will serve you well down the line, especially as you start or advance in your career."

Because so many people work remotely right now, your location has never limited you less than this moment.

Reach out: You can shoot for an internship with an ad agency in New York from your parents' farm in Nebraska, or take on some of your aunt's data entry work for an Australian company from your apartment in Los Angeles.

Create a Position for Yourself Out of the Pandemic

Use your imagination. Is your neighbor juggling working at home with their kids' online learning? Maybe you could take their kids out on nature walks or learning field trips. Do you have a relative whose workplace needs to be sanitized? You could offer to clean in exchange for them training you to keep the books, sort the files, collect client data — *voila*, you just became a business intern.

Listen to the people in your life still lucky enough to have jobs. If the pandemic or the recession have left gaping needs in their resources, you can offer your skills to supplement — for a price.

Work in Contact Tracing

If you'd like to work from home, on your own terms, and make $17-38/hour[190], then contact tracing might be the job for you, at least for now.

You do not need a college degree or experience in public health. You simply take a brief training course and then get on the phone, calling people who've tested positive for COVID, to track where they went and whom they interacted with before contracting the virus. Think of yourself as an infectious-disease detective.

The three skills most crucial to this job: an ability to build *trust*, as you must essentially violate each person's privacy with your questions about their whereabouts, and convince them of the greater good of stopping the spread of the virus; *patience*, as people may react rudely or negatively to your inquiry; and *resilience*, to let the stress of people's struggles that you hear about all day roll off you when you clock out.

Money.com[191] calls contact tracing "one of the most in-demand jobs right now." You can work from anywhere, for any region of your country that has the highest need at this time.

Emily Gurley, a Johns Hopkins epidemiologist, calls contact tracers "part detective, part therapist, and part social worker." She offers a free training course on Coursera[192] for contact tracing.

The Centers for Disease Control (CDC) have posted details on what you would do as a contact tracer here[193]. If you have fluency in more than one language, you stand an even better chance of helping your community while making good money during a crisis.

Internships: Research the Position You Desire

Before You Start

1. **Research the position.** What are its key responsibilities? What required skills,

knowledge and qualities are listed in the posting?

2. **Research the organization.** What is its culture? Its history? Its strategic goals? Make sure you understand what this organization does and how they describe themselves. You can usually find this information on the organization's website.

3. **Identify your most relevant skills and competencies.** Then create individual "stories" from your work experience (such as best and worst moments) that illustrate your competencies in the required areas.

Cover Letter/Email How-Tos

It's Your First Impression on Them

The purpose of the cover letter (even if sent via email rather than on old-fashioned paper) is to demonstrate to the employer that you are a good fit for their organization and the role for which you're applying.

To stand out, it's important to personalize your note for each internship position. The first few sentences should show that you've done your research about the internship and the organization, and should make an employer want to learn more about you. The body of the letter is your chance to pick out a few keywords from the position description and dive into examples of how you've exhibited these skills.

A cover letter is also the first writing sample that an employer sees from you. Make every word count, and make sure the final version is polished and error-free.

Did you know? The majority of employers prefer a cover letter that's 250 words[194] or less.

Formatting Basics

1. Font: Use a 12-point standard font (e.g., Times New Roman, Garamond, Verdana, Helvetica, Arial).
2. Spacing: Set document margins to at least 1" all around. Center your letter on the page and left-justify (rag-right) all text.
3. Heading: Use business letter format[195] and provide a hyperlink to your LinkedIn profile in the signature area.
4. Use formal terms and lean toward a professional tone whenever possible.

Writing Style

1. **Be specific:** Tailor each note to that particular position and employer. This shows the recipient that you're truly interested in the job and that you took the time to research the organization.
2. **Be concise:** Keep it short, to just a couple of paragraphs. Briefer is better! Be clear and avoid using flowery or boastful language. Save the details for the interview.
3. **Complement your resume/LinkedIn:** Rather than repeating information, tell specific stories

and use examples. *The tone should be what you can do for the employer, not what they can do for you.*

4. **NEVER be negative:** Don't apologize for not yet possessing a skill they would like to see.

5. **Proofread, proofread, proofread:** Typos signal a lack of attention to detail.

Cover Letter Template

The following is an internship cover letter template to provide some initial structure and inspiration. Ideally, you'll supplement this template with your own creativity and flair.

Your Name
Email
LinkedIn (hyperlinked)
Date

To Whom It May Concern,

[Paragraph One]
[Body Paragraphs]
[Closing Paragraph]

Sincerely,
Your Name

Mistakes to Avoid

"In a sea of youthful candidates," Mark Slack writes in an article[196] in *The Muse*, "most of your resumes will look very similar."

The article provides practical tips on how to make a unique impression with the fewest possible words; shows how to master length, tone, genuineness, and confidence; and offers ways to shift from college-talk toward becoming an asset at your new company. We've condensed his list of resume mistakes for you here:

1. It's too long.
2. It's overly formal.
3. It sounds disingenuous (false).
4. You're underselling yourself.
5. It sounds selfish.
6. It's full of irrelevant filler.
7. It has too much information about your college.

Sounds pretty tricky to strike the perfect balance between underselling and BSing, right? Yet, it is possible to present your accomplishments in a matter-of-fact tone and still come across as humble.

The best tip we can offer you comes from our own English-major college studies: *Show, don't tell.* That is, instead of bragging about being smart, describe the art or app or product you invented while still in school. Rather than trumpeting your ability to remain calm under pressure, cite the numbers of people you served at your restaurant or shop during a rush, or explain techniques you invented to make customers happy. Lay out the evidence for why you've got talent

— for pity's sake, don't boast about it — and your next employer will reach their conclusions on their own.

Compose a Succinct Resume

Whether you're simply networking or actually applying for a job or internship, a polished resume can distinguish you from other candidates.

Skills and Brevity Count

1. Tailor your resume to each type of position.
2. Employers are interested in your skills, regardless of how you utilized them.
3. You do not need to focus only on paid experiences. Unpaid internships, activities and volunteer positions can often provide you the opportunity to highlight as much, or more, experience than paid work.
4. Employers decide in just a few seconds whether or not a resume is of interest. Front-load your resume, putting your most relevant experience in the top third of the page.

Use Action Verbs

Start off each line of your resume with an action verb. Actions verbs specify what you *know* and what you *do*. Select verbs that precisely identify the relevant skills or experiences you have that match a particular employer's needs.

Sections to Include in Your Resume

1. **Contact:** Name, address, phone, email and LinkedIn URL, if applicable.
2. **Education:** As an undergraduate or recent graduate, this is always your first section. Include your college as well as any other higher education experience (internships, study abroad, significant study away in the U.S.).
3. **Experience:** List/describe experiences most pertinent to the skills needed in a particular position. This includes work you've done as a volunteer, and sometimes even what you've done to assist your home and family.
4. **Additional skills/interests:** Include foreign languages, computer skills, sports, and fine/performing arts. Do not include a long form, objective statement or photograph.

What to List Under "Experience"

1. Within each experience section, list the name of the organization, location (mainly city/state, but if outside the U.S. include the country), your title, and the dates (in months and years) that you performed the work.
2. Use **action verbs** to describe your duties. Rather than saying "responsibilities included organizing," you'll want to say, "organized."
3. Use **bullet points** to list information. When writing bullet points, strive to include details about challenges you addressed, actions you took, and results. Include numbers whenever

possible. Some students use the APR structure (Action, Process, Results) to draft bullet points.

4. Wherever possible, use **keywords** from the job or internship posting in your description of your experiences. Some employers use Applicant Tracking Systems to seek out these keywords.

5. Use **present tense** for ongoing activities, past tense for prior experiences.

Best Practices for Formatting

1. **Keep it to one page:** Use white space to make the resume easy to read.

2. **Use a common font:** Between 10-12 points in size (except for your name, which should be bigger). Times New Roman, Garamond, Arial, and Verdana are all acceptable.

3. **Format consistently:** For instance, if you list your title first in one entry in a section, do it the same way for the rest of the listings in that section. Use consistent formatting across sections to the extent that is practicable.

4. **Reverse chronology:** For items within each section, place your most recent experience first.

Use the Right Keywords in Your Resume

Have you ever heard of applicant tracking systems[197]? It's when a company uses a computer program to filter through applications and resumes, weeding out the candidates who aren't a fit — simply because they didn't use the right words[198].

That's right: your resume[199] could be chucked in the proverbial trashcan before it ever reaches a human's eyes, all because you didn't use a word the system was searching for.

How do you know which words to use? A good place to start is the job description[200]. Read more here[201].

How To Create a Powerful Profile on LinkedIn

Why Bother?

1. There are over 660 million[202] users from over 200 countries.
2. 80 percent[203] of users cite professional networking as one of the keys to their career success.
3. 92 percent[204] of recruiters look here for candidates.

What to Include

1. **Headline:** Make it snappy and unique; e.g., "High-school senior and sculptor offers art-therapy skills" or "Economics major seeking to empower the other 99 percent."

2. **Summary:** Use more than forty words in order to boost your search-engine optimization. Here's where you want to let your personality come through. Include your wishes for your career as well as why those goals, and why you're the one to meet them.

3. **Contact information:** List your name and location. Ensure the email address is one you check often. Include a telephone number. The more ways a potential employer has to contact you, the better.

4. **Current employment status:** If you're not yet employed, consider listing your current volunteer or intern position. Another option is to say, "currently seeking _____ opportunity" or "advertising student seeking challenging employment" to show forward thinking and optimism for the future.

5. **Account type:** Choosing a basic account will suffice for most LinkedIn members, unless you're in the field of human resources or recruiting.

6. **Photograph:** Choose the most professional headshot you can obtain. Like it or not, people will judge you by the smile, warmth, and intelligence that shine through. This isn't the place for a cool pic of you in sunglasses, at a party, or at the beach with your dog. Profiles

with a high-quality headshot get twenty-one times[205] more profile views.

7. **Experience:** First, list any paid work experiences. Consider listing them in an order that most closely matches your career goals rather than chronologically. Keep it honest but inclusive of *all* other relevant experience, including summer experiences, volunteer stints, hobbies and talents.

8. **Skills:** LinkedIn offers fifty from which to choose. If you pick at least five, you'll be contacted by thirty-three times[206] more recruiters.

9. **Education:** Include what you've studied beyond the diploma, e.g., certifications and online learning.

10. **Personalized URL:** If possible, use your full name as your LinkedIn URL; that will make it easier for people to find you. Click the "gear" icon next to the public profile link, then click the pencil message next to the URL. Your personalized URL must be between five to thirty characters.

11. **Edit, proofread, edit, and check again:** Aim for brevity and clarity. Use syntax that's sharp and refreshing, not stuffy or pretentious. Ask a hawk-eyed teacher or family member to double-check your entry before you hit "publish."

12. **Network with people:** Now it's time to reach out to everyone you know: teachers, relatives, family friends, and anyone you've met who's already working in your field. Why? Because especially online, it's all about whom you know and whom they know.

Polishing Your Profile

Keywords: Using industry terms helps people find you when searching on a specific topic or skill. For example, if you're a nursing student, you might weave in such words as "medical," "healthcare," and "patient-centered." However, try not to repeat any words in your profile — instead, summarize or synonymize.

Updates: Posting updates keeps your profile fresh, notifies your contacts of new content, and brings online searches to you. Consider posting interesting articles you've encountered or your own work — blog posts, articles, how-to lists, or on-the-job stories of challenges and triumphs.

Video: Especially for Gen Z, any story that you can tell on video in eight seconds[207] or less (could be yourself talking or images with captions) has the best chance of connecting with and being shared by others.

Activity: Check in often, just as you would with any other social media tool. If you send someone an invitation to connect, add a personal touch as to why. If you receive an introduction or recommendation, be sure to circle back to those who've helped you along your career path. It's not just good karma, it's also your good reputation, which will open doors for you in the years to come.

How To Use Your Phone To Find a Job

If you're looking for your first job[208], you may be more comfortable on your phone than on a job site.

If so, the following job search scenarios may sound familiar. Have you ever emailed yourself the link to a job listing so you'd remember to apply when you got home to your laptop? Or have you ever missed out on a position because you applied too late? We've all been there, but you don't have to be.

Lucky for you, there are a bevy of apps, including Glassdoor's app for iPhone and Android[209], that can help you in your job search and even help you find a dream job. Read more here[210].

How To Capture an Employer's Attention in 6 Seconds

Depressing statistic: Recruiters and hiring managers only spend an average of six seconds reading your resume[211]. (We know, it hurts. But we also noticed that their attention span is even briefer than yours, haha — six seconds compared to your eight.)

That's not a lot of time to capture their attention[212]. That's why it's so important to know what potential employers are looking for[213] in those few precious seconds, and put them in your resumes.

Consider: technical skills, soft skills[214], examples of impact[215], certifications[216], and quantifiable successes. Read more here[217].

How To Organize and Track Your Job Search

If your search requires you to apply to more than one job, read this section for how to keep track and keep your sanity.

When on the hunt for a job[218], it's not uncommon to be applying for multiple opportunities at once.

This is especially true for those of us just starting out in our careers[219]. But multiple applications mean different resume versions[220], various cover letters[221], and many different deadlines to keep track of. With so many moving parts at once, it's easy to become disorganized.

But a disorderly job search process can lead to embarrassing mistakes such as lost phone numbers, confused deadlines, and missed interviews[222].

To help you avoid these downfalls, here are a few tips to help you keep your job search organized.

Step 1: Start with Your Career Goals

It's natural to want to just jump right in and begin filling out job applications[223]. But before you do, it's best to take a step back and get a look at the bigger picture. Your career journey should start with a look at the direction in which you're headed.

Thinking through the career path[224] you'd like to pursue is one of the most important steps to take. How are you supposed to get anywhere if you don't know where you want to go?

Reflect on what you'd like to do and why you feel that's the right path for you.

Start by thinking about your long-term goals[225] as those don't need to be overly specific. Where do you want to be ten years from now?

Then work backward from there down to five years, one year, and six months from now. Be sure to think through your personal goals in addition to your career and finances. Take your family, education, and anything else you value into consideration.

Step 2: Create a Schedule

Now it's time to start building out a schedule[226].

First, identify blocks of time within your schedule between classes, work, and other responsibilities that you can dedicate to job searching. Job searching is a time-consuming process, and it requires regular attention.

Next, build a schedule to complete certain tasks you know you need to get done. For instance, devote one hour to cleaning up your professional online profiles[227] like LinkedIn. Devote another hour or two to preparing your resume[228].

Perhaps even more important than actually setting up this schedule is sticking to it. Let's be honest here: Activities like resume building and email sending[229] are less-than-thrilling tasks. It can be easy to let these to-dos fall by the wayside and choose something a little more exciting to occupy your time. However, this will only put you behind and lead you down a path of disorganized job searching.

Step 3: Minimize Your Job Applications

Looking for a job is often a high-pressure situation[230], so you might be tempted to begin aimlessly applying for any open position you find. But even though applying for more jobs[231] can make it feel like you're increasing your chances, this is actually just a waste of your time — and an easy way to become disorganized.

Go back to your long-term and short-term goals. Narrow your search to only the jobs that align with those goals.

Next, narrow your search down to only the openings that match the level of skill you have. This doesn't necessarily mean that your qualifications need to match up with those listed on the job description exactly. In fact, this will likely never be the case. Job descriptions should be more of a directional tool for whether or not you're a potential fit for a role, so aim for an 80 percent match with the qualifications listed.

Step 4: Track Each Position You Apply For

Here's where things can get especially messy. Applying for multiple positions[232] at once leaves you with a lot of different things to manage. It's very important to make sure you're keeping track of all of the different details as you go along.

One of the best ways to do this is to create a spreadsheet[233]. This is an easy and effective way to help you keep track. Don't worry about making anything too fancy. Just be sure to include basic information such as:

1. Company name
2. Contact details (name, email and phone number) of your contact at the company, in most cases a hiring manager[234]
3. Date applied
4. Deadlines for upcoming information the company asks for, and scheduled interviews
5. Date you followed up after an application submission or interview
6. Status of application: whether you've been rejected, are waiting to hear back, or have an interview scheduled

Tools for this include Excel and the Glassdoor's Job-Search Tracker[235] spreadsheet.

However, setting up a tracking system alone is not enough. You need to be diligent in updating your system each time you take a new action or receive an update from a potential employer.

There are so many different things to keep track of when job searching, but by following these few simple tips, you'll be ready for a more organized and effective job hunt.

How To Interview To Get the Job You Want

So maybe it takes you one hundred queries to get one interview. No one's career path follows a straight line.

Let's say you get the chance to interview for a job that you actually really desire. Here's how to get from the jitters to the offer.

Before the Interview: Preparation

Preparation is essential. Employers immediately can tell whether a candidate is prepared or not, the moment they enter the room. Make sure you're armed and ready to impress them. Do your research and anticipate what questions will be asked during the interview.

What should you research on?

1. **Background and history of the company.** You have to know the company that you are

applying to. If you claim to have a desire to work in that organization but you do not know the basic information about it, your credibility will immediately go right out the window. And don't just stick to the basic information, either — company size, industry and products. Look deeper, such as the organization's goals, vision, its current performance, and what you think of its future.

2. **The job you are applying for.** You should know and understand what job you are applying for, and what it is about. You should have some basic knowledge on the duties and responsibilities that come with the position, because how can you claim to be a very good fit for the job when you don't know what it involves?

3. **Background of the interviewer.** Learn about the people who will be interviewing you, through things like their company bio, online searches, and LinkedIn. This will put you in a position where you will better understand and anticipate the questions that will be asked, and show that you respect them and their time.

You can get your information for your job interview research from various sources. Start from the website of the organization and any articles published about them.

Anticipate and Review Their Questions

Job seekers are advised to make a list of the questions that they expect to hear during the interview.

You may look for these anticipated questions online or ask others who have gone through job interviews for pointers.

Formulate your answers as you envision yourself being asked these questions by an interviewer.

Keep responses concise but detailed. You should go directly to the point when answering. Don't meander or become long-winded, because this has the tendency to bore your interviewers. It may also take up a lot of time, especially when you only have a few minutes allotted for the interview. You might end up being able to answer only one or two questions because you talked too much, focusing on the buildup rather than the heart of your answer.

Do not memorize. There is a danger to memorizing responses. It is possible that the question that will be asked has variations on what you practiced or memorized, and you will be caught off-guard. It's better to come up with talking points, and work around it with your potential answers.

Dress for Success

The term "first impressions last" applies to interviews as well.

Interviewers put a lot of stock[236] on how you come across the moment you enter a room, and a huge factor in that is how you are dressed.

Being "presentable" is no longer enough; you have to dress well, and dress in a manner that any employer or organization would approve of.

COVID Update: Appearance Matters Onscreen

This matters just as much onscreen as in-person ... at least for the portion of your apparel that can be seen!

1. Dress in an appropriate and professional manner; i.e., match up with the job you are applying for. If you are applying for a managerial or supervisory position, you should exude the aura of a manager or a supervisor. There is a rule of thumb that says you should dress "two levels up," or two levels higher than the position you are applying for.

2. Dressing appropriately means you should also make sure your outfit is not too racy. Low and plunging necklines, sleeveless tops, and extremely short skirts are not good options. This may give your interviewers the wrong impression.

3. The default job interview outfit usually consists of a suit, but you can be flexible. Fortunately, corporate and professional dressing has evolved over the years, so that you can dress in a manner that represents your personality while sticking to the office's dress code.

4. The outfit should match the culture and sensibilities of the organization. Check if they have a dress code for their employees and pick your clothes in accordance with that.

5. Avoid loud patterns and flashy colors. They will be distracting for the interviewers. You want them to pay attention to you and your answers, not to the patterns and colors of what you are wearing. Similarly, do not over-

accessorize. Wearing too much jewelry will just be distracting.

6. Clean your shoes. And your bag. Scuffed shoes and a messy bag will give your interviewer the impression that you cannot take care of your personal things, so how could you possibly expect to be trusted with company property?

7. Make sure your clothes are dry-cleaned and pressed. Wrinkly or stained clothes won't look good and won't help you make a good impression.

However, dress comfortably. Imagine yourself wearing something very professional to an interview then throughout the interview you keep shifting in your seat because your clothes do not fit very well. This discomfort will have a negative impact on how you present yourself during the interview. It will distract you away from answering the questions properly.

In short, choose clothes that fit, and look good on your body. Clothes give a boost of confidence, and if you are confident that you are dressed well, you will be more comfortable in answering the questions during the interview.

Bring Your Best Hygiene and Grooming

Wear your "power outfit," one that you picked out carefully that makes you feel confident.

Fix your hair. If you wear makeup, make sure it's toned down and appropriate for an office, not a party. Brush your teeth and style your hair. Even at a physical distance, on videoconference, hygiene matters.

Be *Beyond* Punctual

Being on time during the interview shows how time-conscious you are, giving your interviewers the impression that you have good time management skills[237].

Time management is a soft skill that all employers are looking for in candidates, and a great way to show you have this skill is to show up at the interview venue at least 15 minutes before the set time — even if the interview will be conducted from your desk at home!

Punctuality shows your interest in the job. In addition, arriving early shows that you are reliable[238]. It's about respect, both for yourself and for the other person's time.

Arriving early gives you more time to acclimate yourself with the environment or atmosphere at the venue where the interview will be held.

It's also possible that last-minute changes about the interview will be made, and if you are there early, you'll have an easier time adjusting. For example, the room where the interview will be conducted may be changed. You won't end up going around looking for it if you still have more than enough time before the start of the interview.

But don't arrive too early, either. If you arrive, say, an hour or thirty minutes early, this can make you look idle or desperate. Take a deep breath, get a coffee, and then come back.

During the Interview: Be Attentive

Making good first impressions is not entirely up to your choice of an interview outfit.

The first words you say when you meet your interviewers, your greeting to the people you see in the venue, and even your actions and mannerisms are instrumental for interviewers to develop their first impression of you.

Be polite. Have a smile ready for everyone — and we mean *everyone*, from the receptionist to the other staff members you come across on the way to the interview. You never know, you may be working with them in the future.

The same is true if you are being interviewed with other people. You might also end up working alongside them.

This definitely means that you have to pay attention to your body language. Your posture is very important. Slouching makes you come across as someone who is lazy and sometimes maybe even sick. Standing or sitting ramrod-straight, on the other hand, may make you appear stiff and unyielding ... unless, of course, you are a candidate for a position in the military ranks.

If you have mannerisms such as bouncing your knee, tapping your feet or fingers, or wringing your hands, try to correct them. These are often signs of fear, and you don't want your prospective employers to know that you are terrified of them, do you?

There's another thing that jobseekers forget when they enter an interview room: Turn off your phone. Do not just put it on silent or vibrate, because you may be distracted when a message or a call comes in while you're in the middle of the interview.

If the interview occurs onscreen on your computer, you can also deploy your "do not disturb" function. If using Windows, click on the icon in the bottom right of your screen that looks like a page of text, or "Home," and select "Focus assist" to allow only alarms or complete silence; on a Mac, click on the dot-and-dash menu in the top right corner and scroll slightly up for "night shift" and "do not disturb" options.

Be Authentic

More than anything else, be true to yourself. It's normal during an interview to show your best side, but you can do that without pretending to be something or someone you're not.

If you express your authentic personality, you'll come across as natural and real during the interview. You'll be able to deliver more truthful answers, and the interviewers will be able to sense that.

Try to match the communication style of the interviewer. You have to connect with them, while also making sure your personality is showing. You can do this by mirroring their manner. Be business-like when they are business-like. Try to be more personable or adapt a casual tack when you see that they are going that way. Needless to say, if they ask direct questions, then you should also supply direct answers.

Ask Insightful Questions

At some point during the interview, the interviewer may turn the tables and let you ask questions. Maybe you have a lot of questions running through your head about the job. Go through these questions mentally and ask only those that make sense.

Interviewers tend to remember the candidates who posed challenging questions to them.

Usually, interviewees will ask how much the job will pay them on a monthly or annual basis. They may even inquire about the vacation time and other benefits. This is a natural curiosity for the candidate but, depending on the execution or the way the question was asked, it may make you look like your sole interest in the job is the money.

You should only ask about salary and benefits when you have clearly won over the employer. If you wait long enough, they might even be the ones to volunteer the information to you.

COVID Update: Don't Get Too Relaxed on that Remote Interview

In "The New Rules for Job-Hunting During COVID,"[239] the HatchIt blog advises you to take an online interview just as seriously as you would in-person:

"A remote interview might not feel as real or intimidating as an in-person interview, but that does not mean that you can be any less prepared. Sure, you don't have to put on a nice outfit, grab a nice portfolio for your resume, and head to an office building. But you still need to do your homework.

"If you're not prepared for interview questions, tech assessments, and everything else you'd encounter in person, you won't do well in your online interview. Remember, the post-COVID job market will be competitive. You can't afford to miss good opportunities because you didn't prepare.

"No one wants to hire someone who can't follow instructions — especially online. During and after the coronavirus lockdown, employers will be extra sensitive to red flags. If there's a possibility that you'll be working remotely, employers will want to know that you'll be able to figure things out on your own.

An employee who can't follow directions is even more of a problem when they're remote.

"So, if a job application asks you to submit a writing sample as a PDF, or an interviewer asks you to join a Zoom meeting from your computer, don't send a Word doc or join from your phone."

To learn more about video interview etiquette, check out these tips[240] from EnterprisersProject.com, such as virtual eye contact — looking into the camera lens when it counts — and how to look the part for the job you want. They also recommend you show up with ideas about how you might productively conduct your work from home.

Best Practices After the Interview

Thank the Interviewers

The job interview is an opportunity given to jobseekers to show or demonstrate their skills and other qualifications for the job. The interviewers gave you this opportunity, so you should thank them for taking the time to interview you.

Give a firm handshake before and after the interview. Many interviewers observe how you do your handshake[241]. If you have a firm grip, it exudes confidence, but do not grip too tightly, because it will make you appear tense and nervous. If it is too brief, they might think that you are uncomfortable making long contact with others. Do not be too aggressive with pumping, either, because it makes you look unnaturally eager.

COVID Update: Onscreen Goodbyes

The remote version of a handshake may prove as simple as a big, sincere smile. This last moment onscreen is your chance to reveal your warmth and gratitude for the interview.

You can make a brief note about the interview — e.g., "You really tested my I.Q. with your tough questions," or, "I feel like we would work really well together." Or slide in a personal note, such as, "My dog Fido has been patiently waiting for me to take him for a walk," or, "Now I'm off to help my dad cook dinner."

Let your interviewer(s) know that you will follow up immediately with any requests they had. Do it within an hour if possible, or at the very least within twenty-four hours.

If you feel that the interview took a nose-dive, or you forgot to mention something vital, then an email follow-up can help. No need to beg or apologize; rather, attach an article that might be of interest, or offer to submit a project — some type of value-add — that carries the conversation, and possibly the work-relationship, forward.

What NOT to Do in a Job Interview

If there are DOs in participating in job interviews as the interviewee, there are also DON'Ts, or things that could ruin your chances of landing the job.

1. **Do not speak ill of past employers.** Expect interviewers to ask several questions about your work history, particularly on your past employment. They might even bait you when

they start asking the reasons why you quit or were separated from the company. Do not badmouth your previous employers, not even if they were the employers from hell and your complaints are completely valid. The interviewer will conclude that, if you are able to do this with your previous employers, you may do it with them in the future. You should always talk about them positively, but do not go to the extent of making up stories just to make them look good.

2. **Do not talk too much.** Talking too much or taking too long in providing answers for direct questions will give your interviewers the impression that you have trouble getting to the point. This could also mean that you are just bluffing because you don't know a thing about what you are saying.

3. **Do not display impatience.** Is the interview running late? Just stay calm and cool and wait patiently. This may actually be done on purpose, to see how patient you are. Constantly looking at your watch or letting your impatience show on your face will certainly not earn you any points.

Interviewing for a job is one of the crucial steps in getting hired. You can never really do away with interviews, because all job-hiring and recruitment processes include them. Even a simple conversation with the employer may count as an interview. Observe these best interview practices, and they will help you to land your next job, or even your dream job.

Tips and Tools

Apps and Websites That Can Get You to Work

1. Glassdoor Job Search[242] app
2. Glassdoor's Job-Search Tracker[243] spreadsheet
3. Google Alerts[244] to track specific companies and jobs
4. Handshake[245] 'claims it quickly connects students with internships and jobs
5. HelloSign[246] auto-signature for your email
6. JibberJobber[247] online search tool for jobs
7. JobAware on iTunes[248] and Google Play[249] to compare salaries, LinkedIn profiles, and similar jobs at your preferred companies
8. LinkedIn[250] on iTunes[251] and Google Play[252] for customizable search tools, job alerts, and company information
9. Monster[253] for searching job databases and uploading your resume
10. Resume Coach[254] for tips on and templates for entry-level jobseekers
11. Resume Nerd[255] and Resume Now[256] for free templates and examples of resumes
12. Snagajob[257] on iTunes[258] and Google Play[259] to share your personality and participate in Tinder-style job-hunting (swipe right or left based on interest)
13. Zety[260] for job-seeking advice and examples of resumes and cover letters, for teens and first-job applicants
14. ZipRecruiter[261] on iTunes[262] and Google Play[263] for instant access to jobs

Branding to Gen Z—Characteristics of This Market

1. 99 Firms (no author listed). "35 Generation Z Statistics to Start Building the Future of Your Brand." 99Firms.com, April 2019. 99firms. com/blog/generation-z-statistics/#gref[264]. Succinct descriptions of what makes Gen Z unique as a cohort, what types of marketing appeal to them, and how they view the workplace. The survey culls data from Bloomberg, Criteo, Fast Company, Forbes, Pew Research, Statista, The Center for Generational Kinetics, etc., and puts them in one place. Excellent roundup of fast facts about Gen Z.

2. Desjardins, Jeff. "Meet Generation Z, the Newest Member to the Workforce," Visual Capitalist, February 14, 2019. visualcapitalist. com/meet-generation-z-the-newest-member-to-the-workforce[265]. Tracks differences between Gen Zers and Millennials regarding careers and aspirations, including proclivities toward ultra-connectivity and in-person interactions, diversity and racial equality, saving money and achieving job stability.

Career Day Online, Anytime: Gladeo's Skills Testing, Job Videos, and Career Planning

Want to explore hundreds of careers to discern which one might be best suited for you? Gladeo[266], an online career planning platform, offers personality and skills testing, along with video interviews with real-life people in industries from healthcare to graphic design, construction to defense, media to hospitality. Once you choose a career track, they offer advice on which courses to pursue in high school, vocational school, or college. They even list companies' postings about internships offered, and when possible, refer young seekers to appropriate opportunities. Because they're online, you can access their FREE services anytime, from anywhere.

Challenges Gen Zers Face in Finding Jobs

1. Alton, Larry. "Millennials Are Struggling to Get Jobs—Here's Why, and What to Do about It." *Forbes*, December 22, 2016. forbes.com/sites/larryalton/2016/12/22/millennials-are-struggling-to-get-jobs-heres-why-and-what-to-do-about-it/#4f5bbd284bb0. Summary of trends in social media and the job market from a diverse set of perspectives, from Fortune 500 companies to locally-owned ones. He notes that the Millennial unemployment rate is a staggering 12.8 percent compared to the national one of 4.9 percent. The reasons, he purports, are the following:

   ■ Millennials these days are too confident despite their young age — if they can't find the perfect job with the perfect title, they cease to look for jobs.
   ■ Their focus revolves too much around themselves and what they have done rather than what they can bring to the table and what skills or talents they hold.
   ■ Education, specifically college, does a great job of teaching students scholarly work in intended disciplines, but fails to

teach life lessons such as critical thinking and interpersonal communication.

■ Millennials rarely check their credit scores due to the stress from the 2008 financial crisis and issues of student debt, but this tends to leave them with bad credit, which hinders their ability to get a good job.

■ It has just become more difficult, in that almost every job a Millennial wants requires at least an undergraduate degree.

2. Clark, Dorie. "You Didn't Land Your Dream Job. Now What?" Harvard Business Review, October 24, 2019. hbr.org/2019/10/you-didnt-land-your-dream-job-now-what. Dorie Clark is a management strategist who writes clear, prolific, practical articles on work/life balance, defining and achieving career goals, and managing yourself and others. Here, she shares her own experience of being rejected by every doctoral program she applied to and what she did about that, as well as ways for you to view what may seem like rejection and turn it into opportunity.

3. Flippin, Dr. Candace Steele. *Generation Z in the Workplace: Helping the Newest Generation in the Workforce Build Successful Working Relationships and Career Path.* Published by the author, 2017, paperback, 120 pages. amazon.com/Generation-Workplace-Successful-Relationships-Generations-ebook/dp/B06XC82SFL. The workplace of the 1990s and early 2000s vastly differs from the workplace of today. Not only are methodologies and technologies different, the individuals who inhabit these spaces are varied as well. Explores ways that Gen Z differs in approaches

to problem-solving, communications, expectations, and interpersonal skills, due to the rise of social media. The author provides a roadmap of how to approach differences within multigenerational workplaces. Written for both the Gen Z workforce and for those who employ them, including nonprofit and volunteer sectors. You can also view her book trailer in this one-minute video[267].

4. Monnig, Taylor. "7 Reasons Why Millennials Can't Find a Job." LinkedIn.com, 2017. linkedin.com/pulse/7-reasons-why-millennials-cant-find-job-taylor-monnig. Taylor Monnig, Chief Operating Officer of TMGcore, a company mining cryptocurrency in Texas, suggests seven reasons why Millennials are struggling to find jobs:

- Loss of opportunity: Millennials are well educated, but jobs they could be qualified for require experience, which recently graduated college students don't have.
- A skills mismatch in the job market, where new skills that Millennials bring to the table are not necessarily the ones the job market is looking for.
- A currently crowded labor market makes it hard for Millennials, at their young age, to find jobs that are full-time and fit their skills.
- While Millennials are entering the workforce with better education than their predecessors, this only happens when Millennials can complete college, but due to the increase in the financial burden of college or for personal reasons, many have dropped out. This poses an issue due to

the fact that virtually all employers now require an undergraduate degree.

■ The high cost of living has left Millennials stuck in positions where income stability has become more important than pursuing a career that they are passionate about. The restaurant business, for example, provides just enough money to stay afloat but has very little upward promotion or growth; yet many Millennials favor this because of its security.

■ Millennials believe they are entitled to their feelings much more than generations before them; and as such, a negative attitude such as frustration can eliminate any positive thinking towards finding a job. Millennials need to stay focused and confident as well as flexible and open to change in order to find a job that best suits them.

■ Given the high cost of education, many Millennials have gone into student debt, which makes it incredibly difficult for Millennials to take risks with their career ambitions when first starting out.

COVID-19 and Its Impact on Gen Z

1. Collins, Lois M. "How COVID-19 Dimmed Generation Z's Plans and Confidence." *Deseret.com*, July 1, 2020. deseret.com/indepth/2020/7/1/21307550/generation-z-facing-unemployment-covid-19-economy-college-pandemic. Gen Z was slated for a prosperous economy with plentiful jobs until

the pandemic hit. Nearly one third of Gen
Zers aged 16 and up have lost a job this
year; many students cannot find part-time
or summer work. Because so many young
people worked in high-risk industries such as
hospitality and transportation, they've been
hit disproportionately by the loss of jobs that
may never return. Gen Zers face accompanying
depression, although this article interviews a
few who remain stubbornly optimistic.

2. Mendoza, N.F. "COVID-19: Gen Z workers
are struggling with careers and worried about
the future." TechRepublic.com, July 2, 2020.
techrepublic.com/article/covid-19-gen-z-
workers-are-struggling-with-careers-and-
worried-about-the-future. Mendoza reports
the findings of a survey by CollegeFinance.
com that included 189 people identifying as
Generation Z, to explore their outlook on jobs
and interviews or job application experiences
since the COVID-19 outbreak. The survey
revealed an average decrease in salary so far
of $6,000; that 71 percent of Gen Z said they
fear going into the job market because of the
instability the potential second wave of the
virus would cause; 60 percent of employed
workers believe a second wave would
negatively impact their jobs; and 23 percent
are worried about being laid off.

3. Threlkeld, Kristy. "Generation Z in the
Workplace: The Impact of COVID-19." Indeed.
com, June 24, 2020. https://www.indeed.
com/lead/generation-z-in-the-workplace.
The generation known for its desire for safety
and stability in the job market has completely
lost its footing, reports *Indeed*. The article

cites what employers can do to ensure they do not lose sight of Gen Z as they rebuild their post-recession and post-COVID businesses. According to LeadersUp CEO Jeffrey T.D. Wallace, "The future of America's economy relies on us not leaving Gen Z out of the growth strategy, and the recovery strategy."

DreamJobbing Platform: Find Your Dream Job Here!

DreamJobbing is an innovative company founded by Lisa Hennessy, Alex Boylan, and Burton Roberts — entrepreneurs, entertainment veterans, and storytellers with backgrounds in network TV, digital content, social media, PR, marketing and technology.

They connect Gen Zers with internships and full-time work in an effort to help students find their ideal career paths, as well as offering job shadowing. Some opportunities are open to students outside the U.S. You can enroll for free[268] in their online "Dreamjobbing U" video-based educational platform to access others breaking into their dream jobs, or learn how to create a video application here[269].

Note that the DreamJobbing founders contacted our team with an interest in joining forces — so, tell them we sent you!

Inspiration: More Gen Zers Making Their Dreams Come True

1. Costil, Albert. "25 Kids That Made $1 Million Before Graduating High School." Due.com, December 6, 2016. due.com/blog/25-kids-

made-1-million-graduating-high-school. Covers a global range of Gen Zers who achieved success — as measured in monetary and business-growth impact — mostly through online and marketing ventures.

2. *Entrepreneur* Staff. "Meet the New Bosses: How These Entrepreneurs Under 20 Are Changing Industries." *Entrepreneur*, August 2018. entrepreneur.com/article/317784. Profiles nine Gen Z entrepreneurs: Alina Morse (Zollipops), Moziah Bridges (Mo's Bows), Rachel Zietze (Gladiator Lacrosse), Abby Kircher (Abby's Better), Brennan Agrannof (HoopSwagg), Anton Klingspor (Indicina Ventures), Keiana Cavé (Mare), Zandra Cunningham (Zandra Beauty), and Isabel Rose Taylor (Isabel Rose Taylor). Each entry takes just one long paragraph but the article goes behind the scenes to reveal the pitches, partnerships, and passion behind building these startups.

3. Frost, Bill. "The Fifty Youngest Kid Entrepreneurs in the U.S." Business.org, May 2019. business.org/business/startup/youngest-entrepreneurs. Gen Zers don't want to be given jobs — they want to create them. Business.org has compiled the youngest startup wunderkinds in the country. Includes an inspiring map of all fifty states with names and ages of entrepreneurs, along with brief vignettes about each of the fifty, what business they built, and how. You've met a few of these Gen Zers in the pages of this book, but most you've never heard of, as well as a few sibling teams. Great fodder for career inspiration.

4. Heintze, Alex. *The Generation Z Entrepreneur: Learn from Successful Entrepreneurs and Venture Capitalists How to Develop a Mindset for Success.* New Degree Press, 2018, paperback, 164 pages. amazon.com/Generation-Entrepreneur-Successful-Entrepreneurs-Capitalists-ebook/dp/B07CJQLJMC. For young people who want to start a company one day; 61 percent of high school students and 43 percent of college students say they would rather be entrepreneurs than employees when they graduate from college. But starting a company is by no means easy. So, the author details seven key principles to fast-forward one's career by adopting an entrepreneurial mindset and preparing to launch that venture. The book brings in the advice and stories of successful entrepreneurs of all ages, from Henry Ford to Reid Hoffman, Jeff Bezos, and Richard Branson. Moreover, it looks into the lives of young people hungry to follow their dreams.

5. Obeso, Borja. "25 Successful Entrepreneurs Under 25 Years of Age." RebelGrowth, no date listed. http://rebelgrowth.com/young-successful-entrepreneurs. Profiles include both Millennials who were under 25 when they achieved their dream jobs as well as current Gen Zers: Mark Zuckerberg (Facebook), Matt Mullenweg (WordPress), Pete Cashmore (Mashable), Aaron Levie and Dylan Smith (Box.net), David Karp (Tumblr), Catherine and David Cook (MyYearBook.com), Sean Belnick (BizChair.com), Matt Mickiewicz (SitePoint.com, 99Designs.com, Flippa.com), Noah Everitt (TwitPic.com), Ryan Allis (iContact.com), Jon Wheatley (DailyBooth.com), Neil

Patel (QuickSprout.com), Kieran O'Neill (PSU.com, Playfire.com), Blake Ross (Mozilla), Eric and Susan Gregg-Koger (ModCloth.com), Shama Kabani (ClickToClient.com), Ashley Qualls (WhateverLife.com), Juliette Brindak (MissOandFriends.com), Sam Tarantino and Josh Greenberg (GrooveShark.com), Richard Ludlow (AcademicEarth.org), and Kristopher Tate (Zoomer). While the list tips heavily toward white male Americans, it proves how much money can be made via internet service companies. A handful of these founders now enjoy a net worth in the hundreds of millions.

6. Post, Jennifer. "Companies Founded by Amazing Young Entrepreneurs." Business News Daily, September 8, 2019. businessnewsdaily.com/5051-young-entrepreneurs.html. Citing "age doesn't equal success," Post profiles fifteen companies started by Gen Zers as young as nine.

7. Shannon (no last name given). "18 Amazing Kids and Teens Who Are Self-Made Millionaires." Self-Made, no date given. self-made.io/18-amazing-kids-and-teens-who-are-self-made-millionaires/6445. Article includes several Gen Zers featured in this book, and the blog covers success stories as well as tips on how to write your own self-made story.

8. Ulmer, Mikaila. *Mikaila's Bee To Z Business Guide.* Microsoft Sway, Free downloadable PDF, 25 pages. sway.office.com/Xv4kF72vx77n9GBF. Calling herself a "ZEO" — a Gen Zer who runs a company — Ulmer, who launched Me and the Bees lemonade company at age four, shares tips and

encouragement with young entrepreneurs whom she hopes will do the same.

Job Security: Does It Exist Anymore?

Brady, Justin. "Gen Z Defines Job Security Completely Differently from the Rest of Us." *Quartz at Work*, Quartz, 25 Sept. 2019. qz.com/work/1709843/how-gen-z-will-change-the-workforce.

Gen Zers are bringing about a cultural shift in the work environment where, instead of job security being something employees will search for, employers are beginning to advertise job security as a tactic to gain more Gen Z interest. They've seen their parents go through hard times with the recession of 2008 and their older siblings' enormous student debt. They hear stories of how younger workers are met with feelings of resentment and disrespect.

This all makes Gen Zers wary of the environment they are coming into, and employers must encourage healthier workplace dynamics if they want fresh blood in the workforce.

Additionally, since the increase of technology, Gen Zers see how easy it can be to start their own company and make money online. Jobs need to be more fulfilling to their intellect. Making minimum wage and working long hours doing boring work is not attractive and just will not cut it for them.

Marketing to Gen Z: What Works

1. Beal, Mark. *Decoding Gen Z: 101 Lessons Generation Z Will Teach Corporate America,*

Marketers & Media. Independently published, 2018, paperback, 150 pages. https://www.amazon.com/Decoding-Gen-Generation-Corporate-Marketers/dp/1724080881. Shares insights from in-depth one-on-one interviews the author conducted with more than fifty Gen Zers across the United States, from high school freshmen to those who just graduated college. This book is written as a guide for employers, marketers and media companies attempting to connect and engage with Gen Z. Note that Mark Beale also published 2017's *101 Lessons They Never Taught You in College: The Essential Guide for Students and Recent Graduates to Launch Their Careers.*

2. Koulopoulos, Tom, and Dan Keldsen. *The Gen Z Effect: The Six Forces Shaping the Future of Business.* Routledge, 2016, hardcover, 256 pages. amazon.com/Gen-Effect-Forces-Shaping-Business/dp/1629560316. (Note: This book is also available in a Chinese edition.) One of the most profound changes in business and society is the emergence of Gen Z. No other generation in history has had the ability to connect every human being on the planet to each other, and in the process to provide the opportunity for each person to be fully educated, socially and economically engaged. What might this mean for businesses, markets and educational institutions in the future? The authors offer a vision of the future where disruptive invention and reinvention is the acknowledged norm, touching almost every aspect of how we work, live and play. From radical new approaches to marketing and manufacturing to the potential

obliteration of intellectual property and the shift to mass innovation, to the decimation of our oldest learning institutions through open source and adaptive learning, *The Gen Z Effect* purports why we need to embrace Gen Z as the last, best hope for taking on the world's biggest challenges and opportunities, and how businesses can prepare for the greatest era of disruption, prosperity and progress the world has ever experienced.

3. Pandit, Vivek. *We Are Generation Z: How Identity, Attitudes, and Perspectives Are Shaping Our Future.* Brown Books Publishing Group, 2015, paperback, 160 pages. amazon.com/We-Are-Generation-Attitudes-Perspectives/dp/1612542182. Born at the turn of the millennium, the members of Generation Z are no strangers to today's fast-paced, hyper-connected world. They were born in the Digital Age. They grew up online. Their identities, attitudes and perspectives have all been uniquely integrated with technology. The author shares an insider's perspective on what it means to be part of this unique generation. By exploring the forces that have shaped him and his peers, he gives insight into how they may go on to shape the world.

4. Pew Research. Ongoing compilation of articles on the qualities and experiences of Generation Z. pewresearch.org/topics/generation-z. If you seek to understand more about your age group, what qualities you share, and how you're impacted by cultural events, this is a goldmine of information that's constantly updated. Pew conducts surveys, mostly in the U.S., and reports their findings vis-à-vis

current issues such as immigration, mental health, voting, socioeconomics, politics and religion.

Mental Health on the Job

1. Bell DeTienne, Kristen, Jill M. Hooley, Cristian Larrocha, and Andheri Reay, "How to Manage an Employee with Depression." Harvard Business Review, January 15, 2020. hbr. org/2020/01/how-to-manage-an-employee-with-depression. One in five Americans grapples with a mental health issue. Moreover, "a recent report[270] by Blue Cross Blue Shield found that depression diagnoses are rising at a faster rate for Millennials and [Gen Z] than for any other generation." This article outlines ways employers can learn about depression, perceive symptoms even in employees who don't self-report, and build a workplace that's supportive and sensitive to their needs. The authors suggest allowing flexible work schedules with some core all-hands teamwork hours, breaking up overwhelming projects into manageable tasks, celebrating moments of achievements, and offering further resources through your HR department or referrals; and point out the critical role that relationships and accomplishments play in recovery.

2. Rogers, Holly B., M.D. *The Mindful Twenty-Something: Life Skills to Handle Stress and Everything Else.* New Harbinger Publications Inc., 2016, paperback, 186 pages. https:// www.amazon.com/Mindful-Twenty-Something-Skills-Handle-Everything-ebook/

dp/B01CFGRFJ0. Based on the popular KORU Mindfulness Program, this guide offers a unique approach for navigating your twenties with clarity and confidence and without stress. Tips include how to gain a healthier perspective, get in touch with what really matters to you, and make important life decisions guided by self-knowledge. Includes mindfulness techniques to help manage day-to-day challenges from a calm, balanced center. Geared toward Gen Zers and Millennials, but useful for any age.

3. Schrager, Allison. "How to Weigh the Risks When Choosing Your First Job." Harvard Business Review, October 25, 2019. hbr. org/2019/10/how-to-weigh-the-risks-when-choosing-your-first-job. While it's natural to feel anxious and overwhelmed by student debt, choosing the right path has never felt more crucial to lifelong success. This author argues that you can make the right choice by applying some basic risk management tools to your most valuable asset, your future earnings, by setting clear goals, weighing risks, and choosing wisely; considering features such as under-valued/high potential; as well as trusting your gut feelings.

Millennials and Similarities to/Differences from Generation Z

1. Dukes, Elizabeth. "Millennials in the Workplace: Trends, Expectations, Habits and More." Iofficecorp.com, 2018. iofficecorp. com/blog/millennials-workplace-trends.

Millennials have different ideas about the workforce and what kind of place it should be than generations before them. The 2018 Deloitte Millennial Survey found that Millennials believe employers should, instead of focusing on the financials of running a company, focus on:

- Job generation and career development
- Developing innovative products and services and generating new ideas
- Enhancing the lives of employees
- Making a positive impact on society and the environment
- Emphasizing inclusion and diversity in the workplace

In essence, they are much more attuned to the wellbeing and safe environment of the company than the logistics of running a company whose security is solely their revenue. While Millennials still value company benefits and salary, they place a high emphasis on:

- A positive workplace culture
- Opportunities for continuous learning
- Wellbeing programs and incentives
- Workplace flexibility in terms of hours and location

2. Elmore, Lauren, for Young Entrepreneur Council. "A Millennial's Take on How to Lead The Millennial Workforce." *Forbes*, October 1, 2018. forbes.com/sites/theyec/2018/09/27/a-millennials-take-on-how-to-lead-the-millennial-workforce/#3d174a3e3bb5. Lauren Elmore is the president of Firmatek and a Millennial herself. She writes that Millennials care deeply about the impact of their work and what their company represents

to the world; they are also opportunistic and on the constant lookout for opportunities to develop new skills or grow. Elmore notes the three best ways to manage and work with Millennials in the workforce:

- Give them communication and feedback, listen to their ideas, and recognize their work.
- Give them professional opportunities and help them grow professionally, hold training sessions, and provide them with opportunities to be leaders.
- Emphasize values and culture. There is nothing more fulfilling than a company whose employees share the same values and whose culture is harmonious with yours.

3. Laramore, Lydia. "For Us, By Us: Career Advice for a Gen Zer, from a Gen Zer." Glassdoor, September 13, 2019. glassdoor.com/blog/career-advice-for-gen-z. Laramore begins with the statement that "Gen Z is setting the agenda for what comes next" in the workplace. She calls Generation Z "innovators and rugged individualists" who do require some training. She gives explanations and tips for these "soft skills" Gen Zers need to be successful in the workplace:

- Grasp the concept of time
- Learn how to work in a team
- Develop empathy
- Adopt professional etiquette
- Cultivate networking

4. Rezvani, Selena, and Kelly Monahan. "The Millennial Mindset Work Styles and

Aspirations of Millennials." Accessed July 24, 2019. 2.deloitte.com/content/dam/Deloitte/us/Documents/process-and-operations/us-cons-millennial-mindset.pdf. Describes how to best help Millennials in the workplace in ways that will, in the long run, benefit both employers and employees. From "coaching" Millennials rather than "managing" them, to building in time for play and other projects, this Deloitte article outlines the best ways to support the Millennial mindset to make them more productive in the workplace.

Podcasts on Gen Z

1. Aspen Public Radio, Gen Z Tea podcast. npr.org/podcasts/769539613/gen-z-tea. New podcast by teens, for teens from Aspen Public Radio, rebroadcast on National Public Radio. "In each episode, we share the voices of our generation through exploring why we are so attached to technology, and how social media is shaping the way we think, act, and relate to one another. We are always connected, but at the same time, we're more isolated than ever."

2. St Fleur, Dorianne. "How to Find a Job During a Pandemic." *Fast Company*, June 15, 2020. fastcompany.com/90515718/how-to-find-a-job-during-a-pandemic-and-recession. Two editors from Fast Company interview the founder of Your Career Girl Inc. as part of the podcast series *Secrets of the Most Productive People*. This might not be the time to pursue your dream job, they say; instead, try to create a plan for work for just the next thirty,

sixty or ninety days. Data entry, logistics, and customer service are industries that are actually growing right now. Take advantage of people being home by asking for their time in an informational interview.

3. Hobson, Jeremy, with Jean Twenge. "Recession, Smartphones, Diversity — What Defines Generation Z, or the iGeneration?" Podcast, 9:20 minutes, WBUR's *Here and Now,* October 2018. wbur.org/hereandnow/2018/10/22/generation-z-igeneration-definition. The post-Millennial generation has come of age: as of 2020, it comprises about one-third of the U.S. population. Some refer to it as Generation Z, while others call it the iGeneration. *Here & Now*'s Jeremy Hobson talks with Jean Twenge[271], psychology professor at San Diego State University. See also Twenge's book *iGen: Why Today's Super-Connected Kids Are Growing Up Less Rebellious, More Tolerant, Less Happy — and Completely Unprepared for Adulthood — and What That Means for the Rest of Us*[272]. Atria Books, 2017, hardcover, 352 pages.

4. Watt, Brian. "Job Hunting? There's an App for That." Podcast, 3:35 minutes, WBUR's *Here and Now*, April 2016. wbur.org/hereandnow/2016/04/04/gen-z-jobs-phones. When you think of young people in the workplace, you probably think first of Millennials. But people in the age group behind them — what demographers call Generation Z — are nipping at their heels. The youngest are in grade school. The oldest have just started college. There are some 60 million of them in the country, and as they make their first foray

into the workplace, they are turning to their smartphones for help.

Racial Justice, Black Lives Matter (BLM), and Values

1. Amortegui, Amber and Natalia Clement, "Generation Z Tackles Racial Injustice Online — And It's Not Just for The Likes." WLRN Radio Miami/South Florida, July 9, 2020. wlrn.org/post/generation-z-tackles-racial-injustice-online-and-its-not-just-likes#stream/0. Even during the challenges of safety, health and unemployment during the COVID pandemic, Generation Z has found its voice crying out for racial justice. This podcast from WLRN in Florida surveys several college-aged students who are using social media to plead for a future society in which they and their children can live as equals.

2. Sakal, Victoria. "Why Gen Z Isn't Interested in Your Statements, Promises and Commitments — Yet." MorningConsult.com, June 22, 2020. morningconsult.com/2020/06/22/why-gen-z-isnt-interested-in-your-statements-promises-and-commitments-yet. Provides data from surveys on Gen Z's response to killings of Black youth by police and the Black Lives Matter (BLM) movement, as well as how Gen Z specifically responds to injustice — e.g., they're more likely to purchase goods from Black-owned shops and support BLM protests.

3. Chang, Emily. "The Driving Force Behind the Black Lives Matter Movement: Gen

Z." TheJournalNJ.com, June 10, 2020. https://www.thejournalnj.com/articles/the-driving-force-behind-the-black-lives-matter-movement-gen-z. This article aptly describes the weight of current times on Gen Z and how young people are responding with power: "Generation Z (people currently aged 5 to 25), in particular, has become deeply committed to BLM ... Using the platform of social media, Gen Z has been able to flood screens with posts spreading news, raising awareness and educating others. Instead of posting typical summer beach day photos, teens and young adults understood the severity of this national issue and made conscious efforts to show their support and respect. As BLM posts go viral, its impact transcends beyond one's immediate community and serves to facilitate change on a national level. ... [T]his technology has allowed BLM to gain traction. Many have also gone beyond social media to establish their own fundraisers, sign petitions and participate in local protests."

Videos: How Generation Z Shapes Our World

1. Browne, Brendan. "How Gen Zers Will Shake Up the Workforce/Talent on Tap." Video, 9:19 minutes, LinkedIn Talent Solutions, August 2018. youtu.be/c3rEXxERGng. Interview with Jonah, a Gen Zer, and his father David, co-authors of *Gen Z @ Work* (see below), in which they discuss generational shifts, qualities of Gen Z, and how they will shape the workforce and world. This video serves as a sort of "CliffsNotes" for their book and

provides a rare factual presentation by a Gen
Zer talking about his cohorts rather than an
older person trying to figure them out.

2.   Dorsey, Jason. "#1 Millennial and Gen
     Z Speaker Jason Dorsey Receives 1,000
     Standing Ovations." Video, 16:47 minutes,
     The Center for Generational Kinetics, March
     2015. youtu.be/RcZieFwXZio. Funny take on
     the painful differences we experience when
     older generations try to communicate with
     younger ones. This might be one to share with
     your Boomer or GenX/Y parents.

3.   Morgan, Jacob. The Future of Work University.
     thefutureorganization.com. Videos, books,
     and online courses to help people prepare for
     successful employment in the future. Teaches
     skills such as empathy and thinking like an
     entrepreneur. Morgan does a weekly video
     called "The Future in Five" — a misnomer
     since the videos are just two to three minutes
     each — covering inspirational and educational
     topics. Morgan also has a podcast on Stitcher;
     a particularly relevant episode is "The Future
     Is Gen Z."[273]

4.   Newsy. "How Gen Z Has Powered Protests
     for Racial Justice." June 8, 2020. youtu.be/
     DVTcddlg6tw. Generation Z activists have
     been the first to sign up to take a knee, carry a
     placard, and speak up for their lives, #MeToo,
     the climate, and now racial justice.

5.   Schawbel, Daniel, with Jill Schiefelbein.
     "What Do Millennial and Gen Z Employees
     Want in the Workplace?" Video, 4:40 minutes,
     Dynamic Communication, April 2017.
     youtu.be/DODu8N_JHyU. *New York Times*
     bestselling author, serial entrepreneur, and

Fortune 500 consultant Schawbel, himself a Millennial, talks about research his company has conducted[274] comparing Millennial and Gen Z employees in addressing:

- Why does Gen Z's communication behavior differ from their communication preferences?
- How do Millennials and Gen Zers want to be trained in organizations?
- Why are physical spaces for work important?
- Why do both Millennials and Gen Zers crave in-person collaboration?

6. Seemiller, Corey. "Generation Z: Making a Difference Their Own Way." Video, 9:19 minutes, TEDx Dayton/Wright Patt Credit Union, December 2017. youtube.com/watch?v=cN0hyudK7nE. The Wright State University professor reveals her direct experience of how Generation Z sharply contrasts with her students from just a few years ago — how they crave deeper impact in a culture of driverless cars, personalized medicine, wars without borders, and pervasive social media. She explores historical events and cultural forces that shaped how Gen Z turned out to be inventive, compassionate, entrepreneurial and practical. Cuts to the chase of how it feels to be a member of Gen Z.

7. Stillman, David. "Are Gen Zers More Like Traditionalists When It Comes to Employment?" Video, YouTube/Sarder TV, 3:02 minutes, December 2018. youtu.be/ex5YACitQTs. Interview with the founder of GenZGuru, author of *Gen Z @ Work* (see next entry) and co-author of best-selling books

When Generations Collide and *The M-Factor: How the Millennials are Rocking the Workplace.* He has contributed to *Time, The Washington Post, The New York Times* and *USA Today*, and has been featured as a generational expert on CNN, CNBC, and the "Today Show." Stillman points to similar core values such as paying your dues (75 percent) and loyalty (61 percent would stay 10 years in a job).

8. Stone, Shaelyn. "What Gen Zers Are Looking for in the Workplace." Video, 1:39 minutes, SunWest Communications, August 2019. https://sunwestpr.com/news/genzersintheworkplace. A public relations intern, herself a Gen Zer, shares three key qualities Gen Zers bring to work:

   - They're ambitious and love a company that has room for potential growth for them
   - They're jacks-of-all-trades and really enjoy having their hands in several different types of projects
   - They value benefits such as great salary and paid time off, because they deeply value work/life balance

What Gen Zers Want at Work

1. Alter, Sarah. "What Does Gen Z Mean for Our Workplaces?" *Retail Leader*, Retail Leader, 23 Sept. 2019. retailleader.com/what-does-gen-z-mean-our-workplaces. Recent study asked questions of Gen Zers in the workforce and collected over 1,500 responses to figure out interesting sets of values. Key takeaways:

- Gen Zers are looking to expand their skill set and are always looking for more opportunities to learn
- Gen Zers do not want to be "put in a box," for example a dead-end job with little to no creativity
- Gen Zers are looking for jobs that pay well, or put them on the path to a job that pays well, as they are more in debt than any age group because of college
- Gen Zers have a high level of importance placed on college education
- Gen Zers are more diverse than any other generation, and they actively seek out diversity and use it as a marker of a healthy workspace

2. Cain Miller, Claire, and Sanam Yar. "Young People Are Going to Save Us All from Office Life," *The New York Times*, 17 September 2019. nytimes.com/2019/09/17/style/generation-z-millennials-work-life-balance.html. Gen Zers and Millennials have been called lazy and entitled — but perhaps, instead, they are the first to understand the proper role of work in life. "It's not about jumping up titles," says a woman who launched her own design firm in Portland, Oregon to allow flexible work hours for all. "It's about finding the best work environment." Younger workers are pushing back against burnout, gender inequity, and unhappiness at work; instead, they're demanding time for meditation and exercise — a life. They want to work remotely, with flextime and the autonomy to get things accomplished on their own clock. ted.com/

talks/scott_dinsmore_how_to_find_work_
you_love

3.   Pradhan, Neha. "How to Appeal to Generation
     Z in the Workplace: Q&A with Panasonic's
     Tina Slattery." *HR Technologist*, 9 Oct. 2019.
     hrtechnologist.com/interviews/culture/tina-
     slattery-panasonic-generation-z-traits.   *HR
     Technologist* interviews Panasonic's director
     of talent acquisition, Tina Slattery, to inquire
     about Gen Z trends and what to think about
     when hiring/creating a work environment
     that's beneficial for Gen Zers. Key findings:

     ■ The world is seeing a rise in *contingent
        labor*, meaning that some workers will
        have ups and downs in the level of work
        they receive, and workplaces need to
        adapt to that shift.
     ■ Need to make HR more accessible and
        technologically interactive to introduce
        Gen Zers to workplace etiquette.
     ■ *Micro e-learning* is on the rise, meaning we
        must give Gen Zers a chance to do their
        own research/learning to improve their
        job performance.
     ■ Job and financial security are at the
        forefront of the minds of Gen Zers.
     ■ Review career plans with new Gen Z
        workers similar to an advisor to make
        upward mobility transparent.
     ■ Job culture and skill assessment are
        becoming more important than formal
        education and accordingly should become
        a larger part of the interview process.

4.   Quillen, Abby. "The Workforce's Newest
     Members: Generation Z." *ZeroCater*, June
     4, 2018. zerocater.com/blog/2018/06/04/

workforce-newest-members-generation-z. The author pulls data from several surveys to create infographics that give a quick, clear view into who Gen Z is and how they work differently than anyone in the past.

5. Stillman, David, and Jonah Stillman. *Gen Z @ Work: How the Next Generation Is Transforming the Workplace.* HarperBusiness, 2018, hardcover, 320 pages. amazon.com/Gen-Work-Generation-Transforming-Workplace/dp/0062475444. Ways in which Gen Zers differ from Millennials and how this generation has a unique perspective on careers and how to succeed in the workforce. The authors offer seven distinguishing traits that we list in this book on page 35.

6. Stillman, Jessica. "A New Study of 11 Million Employee Comments Reveals the 1 Thing Gen Z Wants Most from Work." *Inc.com,* Inc., 30 Sept. 2019. inc.com/jessica-stillman/a-new-study-of-11-million-employee-comments-reveals-1-thing-gen-z-wants-most-from-work.html. New study of 11 million workplace comments shows that, "Everyone wants to be paid decently, treated with respect, and have a life outside the office."

However, Gen Zers differ in that they look for companies that take a stand on political issues and are engaged with the world outside their company. They don't just want to be part of a company that's all about profits.

Gen Zers, "raised in a time when the effects of climate change are making weekly headlines, care deeply about the world around them," Stillman says. And more Gen Zers than any other generation (by a landslide) are likely to make employment decisions based on whether they agree with the stances and values of their employer — whether that's the company or just their boss.

As long as employers balance respect with engagement in politics, studies have found that discussing social issues at work has made employees more productive and engaged in their jobs. The first step is always listening to your employees and understanding what they care about.

Epilogue: Where We Find Hope

By Dr. Wendy Leonard, founder of The Ihangane Project[275] and The Hope Initiative[276]

Young professionals today face a barrage of external violence and prejudice, political division, climate crisis, and changing work environments. They also grapple internally with social isolation and depression at record rates.

Despite the reality that Generation Z has every reason to feel hopeless, these young people demonstrate inspiring levels of hope by fighting for the future they want and expect to have.

To demand change requires a belief that a different future is possible.

At a time when the visualizing of their future may be vastly different and seemingly less certain than the imagined futures of any generation before them, Generation Z is actively reshaping what their future will be. This takes courage — and hope.

The research whose work Dr. Kaye Herth[277] deeply informs, called the Hope Initiative[278] and established by The Ihangane Project (in Rwanda, East Africa and Detroit, Michigan) has demonstrated that hope can be described in the context of three important sub-factors:

- Interconnectedness;
- Temporary versus future mindset; and
- Readiness to change.

With these sub-factors serving as an important working definition of hopefulness, Generation Z is the exemplification of hope in the future. The youth of Generation Z are building coalitions, looking towards the future, and demanding change.

Generation Z seems to intuitively recognize that interconnectedness sparks hope, hope ignites action, and action drives social change. Consider the Parkland teenagers who ignited the #NeverAgain movement[279]. They found resolve in their collective grief and power in their united voices to demand an end to gun violence. Recognizing that gun violence disproportionately impacts communities of color, they actively embrace activists within the larger gun violence movement and lend their voices to those who have had less access to influential audiences.

Then there is Jasilyn Charger, a young woman from the Cheyenne River Sioux Tribe who established the One Life Youth Movement[280] with her friends in response to the growing mental health crisis they saw emerging among their fellow high school students. She went on to establish the International Indigenous Youth Council to empower indigenous youth across the country to fight for their communities.

The youth of Generation Z are demanding solutions to the challenges they face around the world. In turn, these actions are driving change and inspiring hope among those of us who have come to believe that the current circumstances are inevitable.

Brave young women like Malala Yousefzai and Greta Thunberg are risking their lives and forfeiting their childhoods to demand that we do not accept our fate as inevitable.

It is the youth of today who are pushing us all to move from a place of complacency to one of readiness for change.

Yet hope will only last so long if it is not followed by tangible actions that nourish this hope.

As a society, it is our collective responsibility to support the charge for social change that our young people are so bravely — and hopefully — leading.

How does "work" relate to Generation Z? Hopefulness — described as interconnectedness, readiness for change, and future mindset — infuses Generation Z's perspective on work.

Interconnectedness is of critical importance to Gen Zers.

Research has shown that the top two most important factors for Generation Z work environments are "supportive leadership" and "positive relationships at work." Some 72 percent of Gen Zers want face-to-face communication at work; 70 percent of Gen Zers value curious and open mindsets over specific skill sets. It is this kind of *innovation mindset* that supports readiness for change, and a focus on the future that comes from hopefulness.

Generation Z serves as a shining light at the end of a dark tunnel that can guide all of us towards a better world. Yet, hope can only be fueled by possibility for so long. While Generation Z is fighting for the future that we all want to see, we must lean in to support them. Generation Zers have clearly demonstrated their willingness to work for what they want.

As the concept of *work* changes, however, we need to take risks alongside our young people — understanding and supporting their vision of the future, ensuring enabling environments to make this vision a reality, and recognizing that it will be them and their children who will live with the repercussions of our actions today for decades to come.

With great hope in your strength and ability,

Wendy

Sources

Most photographs in this book are either public-domain, noncopyrighted images or were found on such open-source platforms as Creative Commons and Unsplash.

Cover
Cover design by Maya Chawla[281].
Cover image: Open-source image by eric-weber-GAVSp-Ex-6ooc for Unsplash, used with gratitude.

Frontmatter
Graphic "From Gen Z to Boomer" used with permission from kasasa.com.

Chapter 1
Three graphics in this chapter used with permission from Abby Quillen at ZeroCater[282] and have been derived from data from adeccousa.com, blog.globalwebindex.com, businessinsider.com, diversitybestpractices.com, forbes.com, huffingtonpost.com, inc.com, mediakix.com, medium.com, thedrum.com thinkwithgoogle.com, and wpengine.netdna-cdn.com.

Chapter 2
Please note that the images in this chapter do NOT reflect the narrators; rather, they are open-source photographs that portray people doing a job described in that section.

Catherine: Photograph by alejandro-sotillet-XPxWx8-Q49U for Unsplash.

Danielle: Photograph by Alec Couros for Flickr.

Jasmin: Photograph by AtlantaMomofFive PX for Unsplash.

Chapter 3

APPAREL AND FASHION

Brennan Agranoff

Photo from CNN: https://money.cnn.com/2017/04/20/smallbusiness/hoopswagg-brennan-agranoff-socks/index.html

Text sources:

https://bisnett.com/meet-brennan-agranoff-hoopswagg/

https://hoopswagg.com

https://money.cnn.com/2017/04/20/smallbusiness/hoopswagg-brennan-agranoff-socks/index.html

Isabella Rose Taylor

Photo by Rachel Merriman: https://atxwoman.com/isabella-rose-taylor/

Text sources:

https://www.famousbirthdays.com/people/isabella-taylor.html

https://missbish.com/15-year-old-isabella-rose-taylor-is-making-headlines-in-the-fashion-industry/

https://www.isabellarosetaylor.com/pages/about-isabella

Moziah Bridges

Photo from mosbowsmemphis.com:

https://www.businessinsider.com/mos-bows-nba-deal-growth-2017-7

Text sources:

https://mosbowsmemphis.com/pages/store-categories

https://www.famousbirthdays.com/people/moziah-bridges.html

https://wearememphis.com/memphian-stories/moziah-bridges-memphian-on-the-move/

https://thefinancefriday.com/2020/06/05/moziah-bridges-built-bow-empire/

BEAUTY AND BODY PRODUCTS

Daniel Schlessinger

Photo from: https://www.kebloom.com/inspiration/inter-view-with-daniel-schlessinger

Text sources:

https://www.fixmyskin.com/about/

https://www.kebloom.com/inspiration/inter-view-with-daniel-schlessinger

https://www.prnewswire.com/news-releases/omahas-lovelyskincom-awarded-patent-for-innovative-skin-care-product-designed-to-heal-while-moisturizing-dry-lips-and-skin-256338331.html

Isabella Dymalovski

Photo from: https://au.lifestyle.yahoo.com/meet-15-year-old-aussie-isabella-dymalovski-with-her-own-skincare-brand-35072855.html

Text sources:

https://millennialentrepreneurs.com/isabella-dymalovs-ki-luv-ur-skin/

https://www.smartcompany.com.au/startupsmart/ad-vice/startupsmart-funding/how-shark-tanks-youngest-ev-er-entrepreneur-isabella-dymalovski-captured-the-hearts-and-help-of-every-shark/

https://luvurskin.com

Kiowa Kavovit

Photo from: https://www.usatoday.com/story/life/tv/2014/03/12/boo-boo-goo-shark-tank-kid-inven-tors/6173993/

Text sources:

https://www.usatoday.com/story/life/tv/2014/03/12/boo-boo-goo-shark-tank-kid-inventors/6173993/

https://www.bloomberg.com/news/photo-es-says/2014-04-24/young-money-seven-successful-entre-preneurs-under-age-17

https://insigniaseo.com/blog/boo-boo-goo-shark-tank-updates-in-2020/

ENTERTAINMENT

David Dobrik

Photo from: https://cwseattle.cbslocal.com/wp-content/ uploads/sites/31326170/2019/08/David-Dobrik-.jpg?w=1024&h=576&crop=1

Text sources:

https://www.businessinsider.com/david-dobrik-net-worth-youtube-career-vine-liza-koshy-2019-9

https://www.businessinsider.com/david-dobrik-vlog-squad-los-angeles-mansion-tour-2020-8

https://www.famousbirthdays.com/people/david-dobrik.html

Gloson Teh

Photo from:

Text sources:

https://says.com/my/lifestyle/gloson-teh

https://www.youtube.com/user/Glosonteh

http://www.poetrytalents.com/about-gloson/

Jeffrey Owen Hanson

Photo from: https://gkccfonlinedonations.org/hanson/ hanson.asp

Text sources:

https://jeffhansonart.com/?v=dfd44cc06c1b

https://www.youtube.com/channel/UCkkrmBeis9tYY-9h9TwxdEGw

https://hswans10.wixsite.com/heatherswanson/jeffreyowenhanson

Jojo Siwa

Photo from: https://www.pinterest.com/pin/7430940072-51093459/

Text sources:

https://www.cheatsheet.com/entertainment/jojo-siwa-net-worth.html/

https://itsjojosiwa.com

http://www.nick.com.au/jojo-siwa/

https://www.celebritynetworth.com/richest-celebrities/
singers/jojo-siwa-net-worth/

Liza Koshy

Photo by Luke Fontana: https://www.whenweallvote.org/
wp-content/uploads/2019/10/Liza-Koshy-Headshot-cred-
it-Luke-Fontana-e1572553463826.jpg

Text sources:

https://www.youtube.com/channel/UCxSz6JVYmzVht-
kraHWZC7HQ

https://www.famousbirthdays.com/people/elizabeth-
koshy.html

https://www.forbes.com/profile/liza-koshy/#72a1414
6502b

https://www.celebritynetworth.com/richest-celebrities/
actors/liza-koshy-net-worth/

ENVIRONMENT

Greta Thunberg

Photo from: https://www.newscientist.com/article/mg
24132213-400-greta-thunberg-why-i-began-the-climate-
protests-that-are-going-global/

Text sources:

https://time.com/person-of-the-year-2019-greta-thun-
berg/

https://www.bbc.com/news/world-europe-49918719

https://www.theguardian.com/environment/greta-thun-
berg

https://www.ted.com/speakers/greta_thunberg

Hannah Herbst

Photo from BEACON:

http://www.hannahherbst.com/2016wired-magazine.html

Text sources:

http://www.hannahherbst.com

https://www.forbes.com/profile/hannah-herb-
st/#11ddda273dfb

https://usasciencefestival.org/people/hannah-herbst/

Jasilyn Charger

Photo from: https://www.womensactivism.nyc/stories/
2228

Text sources:

https://www.fastcompany.com/3059629/these-stu-
dents-are-developing-bacteria-that-eats-our-plastic-pollu-
tion

Text sources:

https://www.earthguardians.org/speakers-bureau/jasi-
lyn-charger

https://indigenousyouth.org/about

https://www.ourclimatevoices.org/2019/jasilyncharger

Miranda Yang and Jenny Yao

Photo from:

https://www.nytimes.com/2017/01/31/magazine/the-
youth-group-that-launched-a-movement-at-standing-rock.
html

Text sources:

https://www.fastcompany.com/3059629/these-stu-
dents-are-developing-bacteria-that-eats-our-plastic-pollu-
tion

https://www.sciencealert.com/students-are-developing-a-
bacteria-to-eat-the-plastic-pollution-in-the-oceans

https://tedsummaries.com/tag/miranda-yang/

FINANCE

Aaron Easaw

Photo from: https://informi.co.uk/blog/7-most-impres-
sive-entrepreneurs-who-are-25-and-under

Text sources:

https://www.maatermakers.com/Ambassadors/Aaron_
Easaw.php

https://fortune.com/author/aaron-easaw/

https://20under20s.com/aaroneasaw/

Erik Finman

Photo from: https://www.thechronicle.com.au/news/bitcoin-boy-erik-finman-says-if-youre-not-a-millio/3325085/

Text sources:

https://www.investopedia.com/news/who-erik-finman-bitcoin-millionaire-teenager/

https://media.thinknum.com/articles/erik-finman-bitcoin-millionaire-interview/

https://www.businessinsider.com/who-is-erik-finman-bitcoin-investor-millionaire-2019-8

https://cointelegraph.com/news/bitcoin-aint-what-it-used-to-be-pioneer-investor-says

Vitalik Buterin

Photo from: https://en.crypt-mining.net/news/sozdatel-ethereum-obyavil-o-vnedrenii-casper

Text sources:

https://www.forbes.com/profile/vitalik-buterin/#17b14e4f75dd

https://www.wired.com/2016/06/the-uncanny-mind-that-built-ethereum/

https://www.crunchbase.com/person/vitalik-buterin

FOOD AND NUTRITION

Abby Kircher

Photo from: https://www.insider.com/teen-tycoon-abbys-better-nut-butter-2016-10

Text sources:

https://abbysbetter.com

https://www.insider.com/teen-tycoon-abbys-better-nut-butter-2016-10

https://www.thrivetimeshow.com/business-podcasts/15-year-old-entrepreneur-abby-kircher-shares-how-she-built-a-million-dollar-peanut-butter-business/

Cory Nieves

Photo from: https://www.crainsnewyork.com/awards/cory-nieves

Text sources:

https://mrcoryscookies.com

http://www.oprah.com/food/cory-nieves-mr-corys-cookies

https://www.famousbirthdays.com/people/cory-nieves.html

https://www.crainsnewyork.com/awards/cory-nieves

Hailey Thomas

Photo from: https://experiencelife.com/article/cooking-up-change-haile-thomas/

Text sources:

https://www.hailevthomas.com

https://experiencelife.com/article/cooking-up-change-haile-thomas/

https://apnews.com/e7613f193cdb8ed8c5e80a5df-73770eb

Mikaila Ulmer

Photo from: https://atxwoman.com/mikaila-ulmer/

Text sources:

https://www.meandthebees.com/pages/about-us

https://www.cnbc.com/2019/07/17/shark-tank-success-mikaila-ulmer-shares-best-advice-for-entrepreneurs.html

https://www.marketplace.org/2020/08/13/youth-entrepreneur-mikaila-ulmer-on-learning-to-bee-fearless/

GAMING AND SPORTS

Kylian Mbappe

Photo from: https://i.dailymail.co.uk/1s/2020/09/13/09/33118406-0-image-a-46_1599985110713.jpg

Text sources:

https://www.essentiallysports.com/tag/kylian-mbappe/

https://www.businessinsider.com/who-is-kylian-mbappe-world-cup-2018-7

https://www.espn.com/soccer/fifa-world-cup/4/blog/post/3566256/france-world-cup-win-proves-kylian-mbappe-is-the-sport-future-king

https://sportytell.com/biography/kylian-mbappe-biography-facts-childhood-personal-life/

Soleil Wheeler "EwOk"

Photo from: https://www.bestsettings.com/wp-content/uploads/elementor/thumbs/Ewok-olhwj30h45hrrwe9m-rxjajfaaz8bfyn4ul9eqdm3z4.jpg

Text sources:

https://www.forbes.com/profile/soleil-wheeler-/#26cf16012969

https://www.cnn.com/2019/08/01/tech/ewok-fortnite-soleil-wheeler/index.html

https://gaming4.cash/soleil-ewok-wheeler-fortnite-pro

https://www.theverge.com/2019/11/14/20964589/faze-ewok-twitch-mixer-streaming-wars-gaming-ninja

https://www.espn.com/esports/story/_/id/26936088/deaf-fortnite-pro-competitor-ewok-makes-mark-streaming-scene

Sumail Hussan Syed

Photo from: https://www.redbull.com/my-en/sumail-joins-og-interview

Text sources:

https://www.guinnessworldrecords.com/news/2015/8/pakistani-gamer-becomes-youngest-gamer-to-surpass-1million-in-esports-earnings-a-391494?fb_comment_id=959837130724429_960306477344161

https://www.famousbirthdays.com/people/sumail-hassan.html

https://www.bloomberg.com/graphics/2015-pakistani-teens-esport-dream/

IMPACT

March for Our Lives Organizers

Photo from: https://www.smithsonianmag.com/innovation/march-for-our-lives-student-activists-showed-meaning-tragedy-180970717/

Text sources:

https://time.com/longform/never-again-movement/

https://www.newyorker.com/news/news-desk/how-the-survivors-of-parkland-began-the-never-again-movement

https://www.theatlantic.com/photo/2018/02/florida-gun-control-protests-photos/553883/

https://www.businessinsider.com/timeline-shows-how-the-parkland-florida-school-shooting-unfolded-2018-2

Desmond Is Amazing

Photo from: https://www.thecut.com/2018/03/desmond-is-amazing-is-cooler-than-you.html

Text sources:

https://www.desmondisamazing.com/about

https://www.nytimes.com/2019/09/07/style/self-care/drag-kids-desmond-the-amazing.html

https://www.moms.com/meet-the-drag-kid-desmond-napoles-20-truths-about-the-11-year-old-queen/

https://www.worldtop2.com/desmond-napoles-biography-age-height-net-worth/

Isra Hirsi

Photo from: https://www.greenpeace.org/international/story/21117/10-things-youve-always-wanted-to-ask-the-students-skipping-school-to-fight-climate-change/

Text sources:

https://www.vice.com/en_us/article/a357wp/isra-hirsi-ilhan-omar-daughter-climate-strike-profile

https://www.internationalcongressofyouthvoices.com/isra-hirsi

https://fortune.com/40-under-40/2020/isra-hirsi/

http://www.citypages.com/news/isra-hirsi-the-climate-activist/561264211

Kelvin Doe

Photo from: https://www.nydailynews.com/news/world/west-african-teen-wiz-tech-scrap-article-1.1214028

Text sources:

https://www.imaginationmatters.org/index.php/2019/07/12/kelvin-doe-boy-created-future/

https://kelvindoe.com

https://www.blackhistory.mit.edu/archive/kelvin-doe-wows-mit-2012

Malala Yousafzai

Photo from: https://www.theguardian.com/books/2019/jan/19/malala-yousafzai-voice-generation-we-are-displaced

Text sources:

https://www.malala.org/malalas-story

https://www.biography.com/activist/malala-yousafzai

https://www.nobelprize.org/prizes/peace/2014/yousafzai/biographical/

https://www.womenshistory.org/education-resources/biographies/malala-yousafzai

Mihir Garimella

Photo from: https://www.post-gazette.com/news/science/2014/07/29/Local-student-a-finalist-in-Google-Science-Fair-for-his-flying-robot-inspired-by-fruit-fly/stories/201407220008

Text sources:

https://singularityhub.com/2017/08/25/this-inspiring-teenager-wants-to-save-lives-with-his-flying-robots/

https://mihir.garimella.io

https://www.cnn.com/2018/02/08/tech/mihir-garimella-drones-tomorrows-hero/index.html

Shamma bint Suhail Faris Muzrui

Photo from: https://shesmagicblog.wordpress.com/2019/01/01/shamma-bint-suhail-faris-mazrui-the-worlds-youngest-government-minister/

Text sources:

https://www.uaecabinet.ae/en/details/cabinet-members/her-excellency-shamma-bint-suhail-faris-al-mazrui

https://peoplepill.com/people/shamma-al-mazrui/

https://shesmagicblog.wordpress.com/2019/01/01/shamma-bint-suhail-faris-mazrui-the-worlds-youngest-government-minister/

INTERNET

Adam Hildreth

Photo from: http://ent12dmm.blogspot.com/2011/04/teen-entrepreneur-adam-hildreth.html

Text sources:

https://www.yorkshirepost.co.uk/business/adam-hildreth-yorkshire-entrepreneur-behind-one-planets-biggest-internet-safety-companies-1748401

https://www.crunchbase.com/person/adam-hildreth

https://www.crispthinking.com/about-us/

https://www.celebritynetworth.com/richest-businessmen/business-executives/adam-hildreth-net-worth/

Adam Horitz

Photo from: https://www.laweekly.com/top-influencers-adam-horwitz/

Text sources:

https://www.daringtwo.com/post/adam-horwitz-from-dream-...

https://www.incomediary.com/adam-horwitz-interview-6-figure-secrets-of-a-teenage-affiliate-marketer

http://adorasvtak.blogspot.com/p/adam-horwitz.html

https://www.famousbirthdays.com/people/adam-horwitz.html

Carl Ocab

Photo from: https://businessmirror.com.ph/2019/02/17/young-innovator-sees-clear-messaging-site-quality-to-boost-digital-marketing/

Text sources:

https://www.carlocab.com

https://www.forbes.com/profile/carl-ocab/#44848609803b

https://designcenter.ph/design-week-philippines-2017/speakers/carlo-ocab/

Christian Owens

Photo from: https://www.dailymail.co.uk/news/article-1302771/Christian-Owens-schoolboy-entrepreneur-making-million-16.html

Text sources:

https://gizmodo.com/how-a-16-yo-kid-made-his-first-million-dollars-followin-5612145

https://www.crunchbase.com/organization/mac-bundle-box

https://www.forbes.com/pictures/ggji45eiee/christian-owens-21/#26da6911a6e9

https://mixergy.com/interviews/christian-owens-interview/

John Xie

Photo from: https://www.bostonherald.com/2011/05/08/file-sharing-company-wins-babson-award/

Text sources:

https://www.hostreview.com/news/101007-cirtex-corp-founder-ceo-john-xie-named-in-businessweek-america-best-young-entrepreneurs

https://www.entrepreneur.com/article/222646

https://www.theadminzone.com/ams/interview-with-john-xie.58/

Juliette Brindak

Photo from: https://source.wustl.edu/2011/08/entrepreneur-establishes-online-community-for-girls/

Text sources:

https://missoandfriends.com/our-team-juliette-brindak/

https://www.businessinsider.com/juliette-brindak-created-miss-o-and-friends-2012-6

https://yec.co/members/profile/Juliette-Brindak-Blake-Co-Founder-Miss-O-and-Friends/e7b8e1ea-292e-4a27-873f-508695cd4b0f

https://www.teenvogue.com/story/juliette-brindak-hyperlinked-interview

Nick D'Aloisio

Photo from: https://www.ft.com/content/0ff589b6-5801-11e7-9fed-c19e2700005f

Text sources:

https://www.crunchbase.com/person/nick-daloisio

https://oxford.academia.edu/NickDAloisio

https://www.ft.com/content/43a05ff4-45b0-11e9-b168-96a37d002cd3

https://www.wsj.com/articles/how-teen-nick-d8217aloi-sio-has-changed-the-way-we-read-1383785217

Noa Mintz

Photo from: https://www.noamintz.com

Text sources:

https://www.noamintz.com

https://grow.acorns.com/advice-from-noa-mintz-who-founded-nannies-by-noa-at-age-12/

https://www.brown.edu/initiatives/pembroke-oral-histo-ries/interview/noa-mintz-class-2022

https://1851franchise.com/young-entrepreneurs-noa-mintz-of-nannies-by-noa-8897

Stephen Ou

Photo from: https://github.com/stephenou

Text sources:

https://stephenou.com

https://www.crunchbase.com/person/stephen-ou

https://www.raisingceokids.com/spotlight-on-young-en-trepreneur-stephen-ou/

MARKETING

Farrhad Acidwalla

Photo from: https://starsunfolded.com/farrhad-acidwalla/

Text sources:

https://kwhs.wharton.upenn.edu/2017/02/career-insight-farrhad-acidwalla-learning-failure-know-ing-take-break/

https://www.entrepreneur.com/author/farrhad-acidwalla

https://www.farrhad.com

Jesse Kay

Photo from: https://thriveglobal.com/stories/jesse-kay-how-gen-z-can-make-entrepreneurship-a-lifestyle/

Text sources:

https://20under20s.com/about/

https://www.prnewswire.com/news-releases/20-under-20s-19-year-old-founder-jesse-kay-to-launch-trendsetters-a-new-podcast-focusing-on-interviews-with-world-class-entrepreneurs-athletes-politicians-and-entertainers-300906665.html

http://dev.vybermedia.com/spotlight-on-jesse-kay/

RETAIL

Asia Newson

Photo from: https://theundefeated.com/features/asia-newson-super-business-girl/

Text sources:

https://theundefeated.com/features/asia-newson-super-business-girl/

https://www.blackenterprise.com/detroits-youngest-entrepreneur-has-been-doing-business-for-nearly-a-decade/

https://www.forbes.com/sites/leahhunter/2017/01/10/the-13-year-old-entrepreneur-changing-the-face-of-business-in-detroit/#469945671f1d

Ben Pasternak

Photo from: https://nypost.com/2016/04/14/this-16-year-old-millionaire-is-living-your-dream-life/

Text sources:

https://www.gruenderszene.de/business/ben-pasternak-flogg-tim-cook

https://thehustle.co/ben-pasternak-nuggs-simulate/

https://en.wikipedia.org/wiki/Ben_Pasternak

Benjamin "Kickz" Kapelushnik

Photo from: http://yonah.org/channel/sneakerdon-benjamin-kapelushnik/

Text sources:

https://www.businessinsider.com/18-year-old-entrepreneur-makes-fortune-selling-rare-sneakers-to-celebrities-2018-1

http://yonah.org/channel/sneakerdon-benjamin-kapelushnik/

https://www.thecut.com/2016/08/benjamin-kickz-sneaker-don.html

Maddie Bradshaw

Photo from: https://ybridgedotcom.wordpress.com/2012/05/29/meet-maddie-bradshaw-a-16-year-old-millionaire-entrepreneur/

Text sources:

https://millennialentrepreneurs.com/snap-caps-maddie-bradshaw/

http://www.digitaljournal.com/article/346724

https://gazettereview.com/2016/03/m3-girl-designs-update-see-happened-shark-tank/

Nic Bianchi

Photo from: http://edgemagazine.com/lighting-the-way/

Text sources:

https://www.bianchicandleco.com/about

https://millennialentrepreneurs.com/nic-bianchi-bianchi-candle-co/

https://www.crossthebridgecoaching.com/news/2020/3/30/living-his-passion-nic-bianchi-bianchi-candle-company

Rachel Zietz

Photo from: https://millennialentrepreneurs.com/stepping-up-her-game-the-story-behind-gladiator-lacrosse/

Text sources:

https://www.dailyprincetonian.com/article/2019/12/zietz-30-under-30

https://thefinancefriday.com/2020/05/22/rachel-zietz-gladiator-lacrosse/

https://kidpreneurs.org/kidpreneur-rachel-zietz-is-building-better-lacrosse-equipment/

Sean Belnick

Photo from: http://www.goizuetamag.emory.edu/winter2009/entrepreneur.html

Text sources:

https://retireat21.com/interview/interview-with-sean-belnick-making-millions-selling-business-chairs

https://www.inc.com/30under30/2007/the-chair-man-of-the-board.html

https://businesscollective.com/how-i-did-it-sean-belnick-bizchair/index.html

SOCIAL AND RACIAL JUSTICE

Akil Riley and Xavier Brown

Photo from: https://eastbaymajority.com/blm-george-floyd-oakland-tech-student-protest/

Text sources:

https://oaklandvoices.us/tag/akil-riley/

https://abc7news.com/allies-in-action-oakland-protest-east-bay-golden-gate-bridge/6365179/

https://www.berkeleyside.com/2020/06/02/how-oak-land-students-got-15000-people-to-march-against-police-violence-on-monday

Amika George

Photo from: https://www.sistermagazine.co.uk/blogs/sister/sister-meets-amika-george

Text sources:

https://www.rcwlitagency.com/authors/amika-george/

https://www.freeperiods.org/press

https://www.evoke.org/contributors/AmikaGeorge

https://www.theguardian.com/profile/amika-georg

Brea Baker

Photo from: https://www.nytimes.com/2020/06/30/us/politics/abortion-supreme-court-gen-z.html

Text sources:

https://www.breabaker.com

https://www.elle.com/author/15319/brea-baker/

https://www.gatheringforjustice.org/brea-baker

https://www.harpersbazaar.com/author/15319/brea-baker/

Hadiqa Bashir

Photo from: http://www.takepart.com/article/2015/10/02/hadiqa-bashir-child-marriage-pakistan

Text sources:

https://womendeliver.org/classmember/hadiqa-bashir/

https://www.un.org/youthenvoy/hadiqa-bashir/

https://www.bbc.com/news/av/world-asia-32776484

http://www.takepart.com/article/2015/10/02/hadiqa-bashir-child-marriage-pakistan/

Joshua Wong

Photo from: https://www.aljazeera.com/news/2019/10/hong-kong-rejects-joshua-wong-bid-election-191029042425967.html

Text sources:

https://socialmovements.trinity.duke.edu/groups/scholarism

https://www.bbc.com/news/world-asia-29457900

https://www.reuters.com/article/us-hongkong-protests-wong/hong-kong-democracy-activist-group-led-by-joshua-wong-disbands-idUSKBN2410C6

https://en.wikipedia.org/wiki/Joshua_Wong

Nupol Kiazolu

Photo from: https://medium.com/youth-to-power/do-not-let-your-obstacles-define-your-outcome-and-dont-let-them-break-you-interview-with-nupol-1f503f8d770f

Text sources:

https://www.teenvogue.com/story/nupol-kiazolu-21-under-21-2018

https://pen.org/free-speech-2020-an-interview-with-nupol-kiazolu/

https://www.newsbreak.com/news/2049313910762/free-speech-2020-an-interview-with-nupol-kiazolu-president-of-black-lives-matter-greater-ny

Thandiwe Abdullah

Photo from: https://peltthepundits.com/2019/02/los-angeles-honors-black-lives-matter-youth-vanguard-leader-in-recognition-of-black-history-month

Text sources:

https://pen.org/free-speech-2020-an-interview-with-nupol-kiazolu/

https://www.teenvogue.com/story/nupol-kiazolu-21-under-21-2018

https://www.teenvogue.com/story/nupol-kiazolu-of-black-lives-matter-of-greater-new-york-explains-her-journey-into-activism

https://blackfeministcollective.com/2018/06/25/nupol-kiazolu-womanism-bye/

Ziad Ahmed

Photo from: https://knowyourmeme.com/memes/people/ziad-ahmed

Text sources:

https://www.juvconsulting.com/ziad-ahmed

https://www.ziadahmed.me

https://www.huffpost.com/author/ziad-ahmed

https://bookamuslim.com/ziad-ahmed/

SOCIAL MEDIA

Evan of YouTube

Photo from: https://www.dailymail.co.uk/news/article-3071408/Meet-nine-year-old-boy-makes-1M-YEAR-reviewing-toys-YouTube.html

Text sources:

https://www.famousbirthdays.com/people/evantubehd.html

https://www.tubefilter.com/2019/10/30/creators-going-pro-evantube-jilliantube-the-tube-family/

https://www.cbc.ca/kidsnews/post/growing-up-on-youtube-evantubes-journey

Evan Spiegel and Bobby Murphy

Photo from: https://www.latimes.com/business/technology/la-fi-tn-snapchat-evan-spiegel-advertising-20141115-story.html

Text sources:

https://www.thestreet.com/technology/history-of-snapchat

https://www.forbes.com/profile/bobby-murphy/#a-31824537ba5

https://www.forbes.com/profile/evan-spiegel/#1891bf-be529c

https://www.businessinsider.com/fabulous-life-and-ca-reer-of-snap-ceo-evan-spiege

https://www.celebritynetworth.com/richest-business-men/business-executives/bobby-murphy-net-worth/

Kristopher Tate

Photo by Sarah Noorbakhsh: https://www.japaninc.com/mgz_november_2008_new-breed

Text sources:

https://en.wikipedia.org/wiki/Zooomr

Loren Gray

Photo by Rory Alwin: https://www.billboard.com/articles/columns/pop/8485308/loren-gray-kick-you-out

Text sources:

https://www.popbuzz.com/internet/viral/loren-gray/dat-ing-relationship/

https://thenetline.com/people/loren-gray/

http://www.mtv.com/news/3169921/loren-gray-tiktok-alone-video/

http://www.iamlorengray.com

Ryan Kaji

Photo by Ryans World/Youtube.com: https://www.romper.com/p/8-year-old-youtube-influencer-ryan-kaji-made-a-whopping-26-million-in-2019-19637872

Text sources:

https://socialblade.com/youtube/channel/UChG-JGhZ9SOOHvBB0Y4DOO_w

https://ryans.world/about/

https://www.indiatoday.in/information/story/who-is-ryan-kaji-why-he-started-youtube-channels-1701224-2020-07-17

https://au.finance.yahoo.com/news/ryan-kaji-anasta-sia-radzinskaya-millionaires-004443786.html

STEM AND TECHNOLOGY

Jason Li

Photo from iReTron: https://www.iretron.com/pages/our-team

Text sources:

https://www.iretron.com/pages/our-team

https://medium.com/promazo/this-student-thought-shark-tank-was-a-scam-when-they-invited-him-on-the-show-now-hes-working-on-30bea51d29b8

https://insigniaseo.com/blog/iretron-shark-tank-up-dates-in-2019/

Omar Raiyan Azlan

Photo from https://says.com/my/lifestyle/omar-azlan

Text sources:

https://says.com/my/lifestyle/omar-azlan

https://rojakdaily.com/lifestyle/article/4145/5-malay-sians-who-are-actually-super-tererrr

https://www.thestar.com.my/sport/football/2020/07/09/a-rising-red-star-for-malaysia-is-shining-in-bel-grade

Shubham Banerjee

Photo from: https://www.inc.com/jill-krasny/shubham-banerjee-braille-printer-funding-intel.html

Text sources:

https://www.shu.today

https://www.smithsonianmag.com/innovation/meet-13-year-old-who-invented-low-cost-braille-print-er-180956659/

https://www.businessinsider.com/shubham-baner-jee-braigo-labs-2014-11

https://www.wwsg.com/speakers/shubham-banerjee/

TRANSPORTATION

Caleb Nelson

Photo by Jordan Allred/The Spectrum and Daily News: https://www.thespectrum.com/story/news/local/cedar-city/

2017/08/03/pedaling-ahead-cedar-city-teen-launch-es-pedicab-company/536748001/

Text sources:

https://www.romeosrickshaws.com

https://www.thespectrum.com/story/news/local/cedar-city/2017/08/03/pedaling-ahead-cedar-city-teen-launch-es-pedicab-company/536748001/

https://www.ksl.com/article/45928171/pedaling-ahead-cedar-city-teen-launches-rickshaw-company

George Matus

Photo by Steve Griffin/Deseret News: https://www.deseret.com/2019/5/25/20674230/prodigy-founder-taking-utah-s-teal-drones-to-unexplored-heights#george-matus-who-launched-teal-drones-as-a-teenager-in-2014-pilots-one-of-his-drones-outside-the-companys-offices-in-murray-on-monday-may-13-2019-the-company-is-set-to-unveil-a-just-inked-deal-with-the-u-s-army-to-develop-a-short-r-ange-reconnaissance-drone-that-service-members-can-carry-in-a-backpack-and-deploy-as-needed-in-the-battle-field

Text sources:

https://tealdrones.com/about/

https://www.forbes.com/profile/george-matus/#1ee5dc-226c1b

https://everipedia.org/wiki/lang_en/george-matus

Ray Land

Photo from: https://www.inc.com/30under30/darren-dahl/ray-land-founder-of-fabulous-coach-lines.html

Text sources:

https://www.linkedin.com/in/itsrayland/

https://www.inc.com/30under30/darren-dahl/ray-land-founder-of-fabulous-coach-lines.html

http://rattlernation.blogspot.com/2014/09/fabulous-coach-lines-had-5m-insurance.html

https://www.forbes.com/sites/theyec/2013/05/06/an-nouncing-a-video-live-chat-with-ray-land-of-fabulous-coach-lines/#70b99f63e52a

https://www.businessinsider.com/meet-yecs-ray-land-president-and-ceo-of-fabulous-coach-lines-on-startu-plab-2013-5

https://www.gainesville.com/article/LK/20140720/News/604152435/GS

TRAVEL AND REAL ESTATE

Alex Hodara

Photo from: https://www.bostonherald.com/2009/08/24/renting-to-college-crowd/

Text sources:

http://www.bu.edu/questrom/profile/alex-hodara/

https://www.linkedin.com/in/alexhodara/

https://www.forbes.com/pictures/mhj45gjkk/alex-hoda-ra-owner-hodara-real-estate-group-llc-24/#4ecc960e4830

https://www.under30ceo.com/tag/hodara-real-es-tate-group/

https://www.bisnow.com/national/news/commercial-re-al-estate/10-young-real-estate-superstars-to-keep-an-eye-out-for-51983#0

Bella Tipping

Photo by Paige Williams: https://www.dailyliberal.com.au/story/5003177/beaming-bella-proud-to-be-chosen-as-ba-tonbearer-for-relay/

Text sources:

https://www.smh.com.au/business/small-business/is-this-australias-youngest-entrepreneur-20150917-gjojai.html

https://www.girlmuseum.org/girl-entrepreneurs-bella-tip-ping/

https://millennialentrepreneurs.com/bella-tipping-found-er-of-kidzcationz-com/

http://fortune.com/2016/09/15/18-entrepreneurs-un-der-18-teen-business/

https://www.kebloom.com/inspiration/2018/8/23/inter-view-with-bella-tipping

https://www.kebloom.com/inspiration/2018/8/23/inter-view-with-bella-tipping

Chapter 4
Sources are listed in the text and hyperlinked in the ebook.

Epilogue
https://www.thenation.com/article/how-the-never-again-movement-is-disrupting-gun-politics/

https://www.pewresearch.org/fact-tank/2019/01/17/where-millennials-end-and-generation-z-begins/

https://www.dosomething.org/us/articles/7-young-indig-enous-activists-standing-up-for-their-communities

https://www.prnewswire.com/news-releases/fail-ure-drives-innovation-according-to-ey-survey-on-gen-z-300714436.html

https://www.inc.com/ryan-jenkins/the-2019-workplace-7-ways-generation-z-will-shape-it.html

https://www.inc.com/ryan-jenkins/72-percent-of-genera-tion-z-want-this-communication-at-work.html

About the Authors
Sanam Yusuf photograph courtesy of Sanam Yusuf.
Suzanne Skees photograph by Guy Viau.

Endnotes

1   https://www.kasasa.com/articles/generations/gen-x-gen-y-gen-z

2   https://www.myjobstories.org/

3   https://projectinvent.org/

4   https://www.bcg.com/

5   https://www.theatlantic.com/business/archive/2015/10/the-recession-hurt-americans-retirement-accounts-more-than-everyone-thought/410791

6   https://genhq.com/gen-z-2017

7   https://www.deseret.com/indepth/2020/7/1/21307550/generation-z-facing-unemployment-covid-19-economy-college-pandemic

8   https://www.plansponsor.com/gen-z-outpacing-age-groups-saving

9   http://3pur2814p18t46fuop22hvvu.wpengine.netdna-cdn.com/wp-content/uploads/2017/04/The-State-of-Gen-Z-2017-White-Paper-c-2017-The-Center-for-Generational-Kinetics.pdf

10 https://www.thedrum.com/news/2017/01/26/new-gen-z-study-explains-pivotal-generation-marketers-and-brands

11 https://www.amazon.com/Marketing-Millennials-Influential-Generation-Consumers/dp/0814433227

12 Ibid.

13 Find these stories in the MY JOB book series at suzanneskees.com.

14 Skees.org

15 See https://www.ncbi.nlm.nih.gov/pmc/articles/PMC6567908 and https://health.usnews.com/wellness/articles/health-effects-of-unemployment.

16   https://www.businessinsider.com/how-gen-z-feels-about-george-floyd-protests-2020-6

17   https://time.com/3858309/attention-spans-goldfish

18   See https://mediakix.com/blog/the-generation-z-statistics-you-should-know and https://www.pewsocialtrends.org/essay/on-the-cusp-of-adulthood-and-facing-an-uncertain-future-what-we-know-about-gen-z-so-far.

19   https://www.ypulse.com/article/2020/05/06/gen-z-millennials-5-favorite-social-media-platforms-now

20   https://www.thedrum.com/news/2017/01/26/new-gen-z-study-explains-pivotal-generation-marketers-and-brands

21   https://www.forbes.com/sites/kaytiezimmerman/2017/12/17/make-way-for-generation-z-entrepreneurs-saying-no-to-college/#7d02805d47a6

22   https://zerocater.com/blog/2018/06/04/workforce-newest-members-generation-z

23   https://www.quill.com/blog/authors/abby-quillen.html

24   https://www.amazon.com/Gen-Work-Generation-Transforming-Workplace/dp/0062475444

25   https://www.inc.com/jessica-stillman/a-new-study-of-11-million-employee-comments-reveals-1-thing-gen-z-wants-most-from-work.html

26   We, Suzanne and Sanam, surveyed over one hundred members of Gen Z to ask about their views about work and goals for their careers. While not a scientific study in any way, our survey did receive responses from twenty states as well as the District of Columbia (D.C.) across the U.S., along with ten other countries, from Gen Zers in a wide range of jobs. We wanted real Gen Zers to talk about their experiences—rather than rely on what supposed "experts" say—and that's why Chapters 1 and 2 resound with their voices and stories.

27   https://www.amazon.com/Future-Work-Attract-Competitive-Organization/dp/1118877241

28   https://www.qualityinfo.org/-/talking-tenure-a-look-at-generational-job-hopping

29 https://www.urbanoutdooroutreach.org/

30 https://www.businessnewsdaily.com/5051-young-entrepreneurs.html

31 https://due.com/blog/25-kids-made-1-million-graduating-high-school/

32 https://www.entrepreneur.com/article/317784

33 https://www.instagram.com/myjobstories/

34 https://www.myjobstories.org/

35 https://hoopswagg.com/

36 https://petparty.co/

37 https://www.isabellarosetaylor.com/

38 https://www.mosbowsmemphis.com/

39 https://www.fixmyskin.com/

40 http://www.luvurskin.com.au/

41 https://www.heraldsun.com.au/leader/inner-south/teen-isabella-dymalovski-focused-on-growing-cosmetics-business-luv-ur-skin/news-story/4ac82b4162220beb3e86948da852dc14

42 https://www.facebook.com/BooBooGooOfficial/

43 https://www.youtube.com/channel/UCmh5gdwCx6lN7gEC20leNVA

44 https://socialblade.com/youtube/c/daviddobrik

45 http://www.glosonblog.com/

46 https://youtu.be/N_m7gQAGVuo

47 https://says.com/my/lifestyle/gloson-teh

48 https://www.jeffhansonart.com/

49 https://itsjojosiwa.com/

50 https://itsjojosiwa.com/

51 https://www.youtube.com/channel/UCBL8Bg52P8vocka6eTqgkyQ

52 http://www.nick.com.au/jojo-siwa/

53 https://www.youtube.com/channel/UCxSz6JVYmzVhtkraHWZC7HQ

54 https://www.streamys.org/

55 https://www.fox.com/teen-choice/

56 https://www.kidschoiceawards.com/

57 https://www.forbes.com/
pictures/5bd8d2c3a7ea4370591591f4/2019-30-under-
30-hollywoo/?sh=7ed430c638cc

58 https://time.com/5626827/the-25-most-influential-
people-on-the-internet/

59 https://www.celebritynetworth.com/richest-celebrities/
actors/liza-koshy-net-worth/

60 https://www.fridaysforfuture.org/

61 http://www.hannahherbst.com/

62 http://www.ourclimatevoices.org/2019/jasilyncharger

63 https://www.biocellection.com/

64 https://www.maatermakers.com/Ambassadors/Aaron_
Easaw.php

65 https://20under20s.com/aaroneasaw/

66 https://www.investopedia.com/news/who-erik-finman-
bitcoin-millionaire-teenager/

67 https://www.theguardian.com/technology/2018/
jun/13/meet-erik-finman-the-teenage-bitcoin-millionaire

68 https://vitalik.ca/

69 https://www.forbes.com/richest-in-
cryptocurrency/#b96e1c91d496

70 https://abbysbetter.com/

71 http://www.mrcoryscookies.com/

72 http://www.thehappyorg.org/

73 https://www.youtube.com/user/haileteenvegan

74 https://www.meandthebees.com/pages/my-family-hive

75 https://www.youtube.com/
watch?v=rAI7PzoiSSU&feature=youtu.be

76 https://www.cnbc.com/2017/01/12/3-lessons-from-
the-12-year-old-ceo-on-shark-tank.html

77 https://www.forbes.com/sites/toriutley/2016/04/21/
what-millennials-can-learn-about-entrepreneurship-
from-11-year-old-ceo-mikaila-ulmer/#4792dc697619

78 http://time.com/5003930/most-influential-teens-2017/

79 https://www.youtube.com/channel/UCiRikFSmQSgv15G9x9DrFmw

80 https://kylianmbappe.com/en/

81 https://www.cnbc.com/2018/07/02/kylian-mbappe-went-from-a-poor-paris-suburb-to-world-cup-star.html

82 https://gaming4.cash/soleil-ewok-wheeler-fortnite-pro

83 https://www.guinnessworldrecords.com/news/2015/8/pakistani-gamer-becomes-youngest-gamer-to-surpass-1million-in-esports-earnings-a-391494?fb_comment_id=959837130724429_960306477344161

84 https://www.youtube.com/watch?v=CoX_-eX2ByM

85 http://www.guinnessworldrecords.com/news/2015/8/pakistani-gamer-becomes-youngest-gamer-to-surpass-1million-in-esports-earnings-a-391494

86 https://www.neveragain.com/

87 https://en.wikipedia.org/wiki/List_of_school_shootings_in_the_United_States

88 https://www.businessinsider.com/timeline-shows-how-the-parkland-florida-school-shooting-unfolded-2018-2

89 https://www.nytimes.com/2018/03/14/us/school-walkout.html

90 https://www.fastcompany.com/90306922/parkland-shooting-one-year-later-where-are-the-survivors-now

91 https://desmondisamazing.com/

92 https://strikewithus.org/

93 https://www.vice.com/en_us/article/a357wp/isra-hirsi-ilhan-omar-daughter-climate-strike-profile

94 https://www.imaginationmatters.org/index.php/2019/07/12/kelvin-doe-boy-created-future/

95 https://www.tedxteen.com/speakers/kevin-doe

96 https://www.malala.org/

97 https://www.amazon.com/Am-Malala-Stood-Education-Taliban-ebook/dp/B00CH3DBNQ

98 https://mihir.garimella.io/

99 http://mihir.garimella.io/

100 https://www.forbesmiddleeast.com/list/arab-30-
     under-30-2018

101 https://www.dubitlimited.com/

102 https://www.crispthinking.com/

103 https://en.wikipedia.org/wiki/Guinness_Book_of_
     Records

104 https://www.incomediary.com/adam-horwitz-interview-
     6-figure-secrets-of-a-teenage-affiliate-marketer

105 https://www.incomediary.com/adam-horwitz-interview-
     6-figure-secrets-of-a-teenage-affiliate-marketer

106 https://www.carlocab.com/

107 https://offshoring.com.ph/carl-ocab-internet-marketing-
     services/

108 https://www.crunchbase.com/organization/mac-
     bundle-box

109 https://gizmodo.com/how-a-16-yo-kid-made-his-first-
     million-dollars-followin-5612145

110 https://billing.cirtex.com/

111 https://www.taskade.com/

112 https://missoandfriends.com/

113 https://youtu.be/pDq56rUTumk

114 https://en.wikipedia.org/wiki/Summly

115 https://www.crunchbase.com/organization/sphere-
     knowledge

116 https://en.wikipedia.org/wiki/Li_Ka-Shing

117 http://www.nanniesbynoa.com/

118 https://stephenou.com/

119 http://www.rockstahmedia.com/

120 https://20under20s.com/

121 https://thriveglobal.com/stories/jesse-kay-how-gen-z-
     can-make-entrepreneurship-a-lifestyle/

122 https://prettybrowngirl.com/i-see-me-pretty-brown-
     girlpreneurs/asia-newson-founder-super-business-girl/

123 https://eatnuggs.com/

124 https://techcrunch.com/2020/07/09/nuggs-rebrands-as-simulate-with-new-cash-a-new-cto-and-an-expanded-line-of-faux-meat-foods/

125 http://sneakerdon.com/

126 https://www.forumdaily.com/en/kak-amerikanskij-shkolnik-preuspel-v-biznese-pereprodazhi-krossovok/

127 https://www.creativechild.com/manufacturers/view/m3-girl-designs-llc

128 https://www.amazon.com/Maddie-Bradshaws-You-Start-Business/dp/0615387586

129 http://www.digitaljournal.com/article/346724

130 https://www.bianchicandleco.com/

131 http://www.gladiatorlacrosse.com/

132 https://www.entrepreneur.com/article/317784

133 https://www.bizchair.com/

134 https://retireat21.com/interview/interview-with-sean-belnick-making-millions-selling-business-chairs

135 https://abc7news.com/allies-in-action-oakland-protest-east-bay-golden-gate-bridge/6365179/

136 https://www.wsj.com/articles/home-from-college-old-friends-become-protest-leaders-11591790402

137 https://www.freeperiods.org/

138 https://www.gatheringforjustice.org/justiceleaguenyc

139 http://www.takepart.com/article/2015/10/02/hadiqa-bashir-child-marriage-pakistan

140 https://socialmovements.trinity.duke.edu/groups/scholarism

141 https://www.dosomething.org/us/campaigns/vote-2000

142 https://www.blmla.org/

143 http://www.blacklivesmatteratschool.com/

144 https://www.juvconsulting.com/

145 https://www.youtube.com/user/EvanTubeHD

146 http://www.youtube.com/user/EvanTubeHD

147 https://www.snapchat.com/

148 https://www.reddit.com/r/EVERIP/ comments/7n489w/kristopher_tate_explains_everip_at_ tokyo_meetup/

149 https://angel.co/company/connectfree-k-k

150 https://www.tiktok.com/@lorengray

151 https://en.wikipedia.org/wiki/2016_Teen_Choice_ Awards

152 https://en.wikipedia.org/wiki/Shorty_Awards

153 https://www.youtube.com/channel/ UChGJGhZ9SOOHvBB0Y4DOO_w

154 https://www.youtube.com/channel/ UChGJGhZ9SOOHvBB0Y4DOO_w

155 https://socialblade.com/youtube/channel/ UChGJGhZ9SOOHvBB0Y4DOO_w

156 https://www.theverge.com/2016/12/22/14031288/ ryan-toys-review-biggest-youngest-youtube-star-millions

157 https://www.forbes.com/sites/ dawnchmielewski/2020/02/28/how-ryans-youtube-playdate-created-an-accidental-eight-year-old-millionaire/?sh=2c67e7fa3fe0

158 https://www.truthinadvertising.org/ryan-toysreview-database

159 https://www.iretron.com/

160 https://www.braigolabs.com/

161 https://www.romeosrickshaws.com/

162 https://www.romeosrickshaws.com/

163 https://tealdrones.com/

164 http://thielfellowship.org/

165 https://youtu.be/xAzpA6hFINk

166 https://busride.com/businessweek-names-land-finalist-on-young-entrepreneurs-list

167 https://www.gainesville.com/article/LK/20140720/ News/604152435/GS

168 https://www.inc.com/30under30/darren-dahl/ray-land-founder-of-fabulous-coach-lines.html

169 https://www.hodararealestate.com/

170 http://www.bu.edu/questrom/profile/alex-hodara/

171 https://www.brighthub.com/money/home-buying/articles/107288.aspx

172 https://www.under30ceo.com/online-reality-show-for-young-entrepreneurs/#:~:text=%E2%80%9CMaking%20Moves%E2%80%9D%20is%20an%20online,no%20loans%20or%20outside%20investment.

173 https://www.hodararealestate.com/

174 https://www.forbes.com/pictures/mhj45gjkk/alex-hodara-owner-hodara-real-estate-group-llc-24/#4ecc960e4830

175 http://kidzcationz.com/

176 http://fortune.com/2016/09/15/18-entrepreneurs-under-18-teen-business/

177 https://www.kebloom.com/inspiration/2018/8/23/interview-with-bella-tipping

178 https://www.deseret.com/indepth/2020/7/1/21307550/generation-z-facing-unemployment-covid-19-economy-college-pandemic

179 https://collegefinance.com/blog/gen-z-career-outlook-after-covid-19

180 https://www.pewresearch.org/fact-tank/2020/06/30/unemployment-rate-is-higher-than-officially-recorded-more-so-for-women-and-certain-other-groups/?utm_source=AdaptiveMailer&utm_medium=email&utm_campaign=2020-06-30%20Unemployment%20Rate%20Adjusted%20FT%20Heads%20Up%20Note-&org=982&lvl=100&ite=6544&lea=1445558&ctr-=0&par=1&trk=

181 https://www.theguardian.com/us-news/2020/jul/06/gen-z-covid-19-financial-crisis-lasting-scars

182 https://www.theladders.com/career-advice/generation-z-careers-coronavirus-pandemic

183 https://learn.joinhandshake.com/students/how-to-get-an-internship-or-job-when-hiring-is-all-virtual/

184 https://www.coursera.org/

185 https://www.edx.org/

186 https://www.khanacademy.org/

187 https://www.classcentral.com/

188 https://www.coursera.org/government/workforce-recovery

189 https://www.seattletimes.com/life/sometimes-you-need-to-let-go-of-one-dream-to-get-to-the-new-dream-millennials-give-advice-to-generation-z/

190 https://www.cnbc.com/2020/06/02/how-to-become-a-contact-tracer-one-of-the-fastest-growing-jobs-in-us.html

191 https://money.com/coronavirus-contract-tracing-jobs/

192 https://www.coursera.org/learn/covid-19-contact-tracing?edocomorp=covid-19-contact-tracing

193 https://www.cdc.gov/coronavirus/2019-ncov/downloads/php/contact-tracing/COVID19-contact-tracer-508.pdf

194 https://www.saddleback.edu/uploads/jobs/documents/The2011OrangeCountyResumeSurvey.pdf

195 https://writing.wisc.edu/Handbook/Bus/BusinessLetter.html

196 Slack, Mark. "7 Cover Letter Mistakes Entry-Level Candidates Make—and How to Fix Them Now." The Muse, 2019. themuse.com/advice/7-cover-letter-mistakes-entrylevel-candidates-makeand-how-to-fix-them-now

197 https://www.glassdoor.com/blog/gaming-applicant-tracking-systems/

198 https://www.glassdoor.com/blog/gaming-applicant-tracking-systems/

199 https://www.glassdoor.com/blog/anatomy-perfect-resume/

200 https://www.glassdoor.com/blog/how-to-read-job-description/

201 https://www.glassdoor.com/blog/how-to-write-a-cover-letter-resume/

202 https://about.linkedin.com/

203 https://blog.linkedin.com/2017/april/13/introducing-a-smarter-way-to-message-and-build-meaningful-relationships-on-linkedin

204 https://www.adweek.com/digital/survey-96-of-recruiters-use-social-media-to-find-high-quality-candidates/

205 https://www.inc.com/john-nemo/how-to-make-your-linkedin-profile-20x-more-appealing-according-to-science.html

206 https://blog.linkedin.com/2016/08/03/5-steps-to-improve-your-linkedin-profile-in-minutes-

207 https://www.entrepreneur.com/article/334791

208 https://www.glassdoor.com/blog/the-surprising-first-jobs-of-14-successful-executives/

209 https://www.glassdoor.com/blog/glassdoor-job-search-app/

210 https://www.glassdoor.com/blog/glassdoor-job-search-app/

211 https://www.glassdoor.com/blog/scanning-resumes/

212 https://www.glassdoor.com/blog/certifications-impress-recruiters/

213 https://www.glassdoor.com/blog/scanning-resumes/

214 https://www.glassdoor.com/blog/improve-your-chances-of-being-hired/

215 https://www.glassdoor.com/blog/types-of-resumes-thatll-get-your-foot-in-the-door/

216 https://www.glassdoor.com/blog/certifications-impress-recruiters/

217 https://www.glassdoor.com/blog/informed-candidate-survey/

218 https://www.glassdoor.com/blog/guide/how-to-find-a-job-in-a-new-city/

219 https://www.glassdoor.com/blog/must-have-entry-level-worker-skills/

220 https://www.glassdoor.com/blog/guide/how-to-write-a-resume/

221 https://www.glassdoor.com/blog/guide/how-to-write-a-cover-letter/

222 https://www.glassdoor.com/blog/interview-horror-stories/

223 https://www.glassdoor.com/blog/diversity-in-a-job-application/

224 https://www.glassdoor.com/blog/wrong-career-path-3-ways-track/

225 https://www.glassdoor.com/blog/4-steps-to-determine/

226 https://www.glassdoor.com/blog/5-tips-times-schedule-interview/

227 https://www.glassdoor.com/blog/clean-social-media-presence-job/

228 https://www.glassdoor.com/blog/what-hiring-managers-expect-on-resumes-now/

229 https://www.glassdoor.com/blog/how-to-follow-up-after-an-interview/

230 https://www.glassdoor.com/blog/relax-at-work/

231 https://www.glassdoor.com/blog/guide/how-to-apply-for-a-job/

232 https://www.glassdoor.com/blog/guide/how-to-apply-for-a-job/

233 https://www.glassdoor.com/blog/job-search-tracker/

234 https://www.glassdoor.com/blog/what-hiring-managers-expect-on-resumes-now/

235 https://www.glassdoor.com/blog/job-search-tracker/

236 http://www.expectingchange.com/why-first-impressions-are-so-important-in-a-job-interview/

237 https://www.cleverism.com/complete-guide-to-time-management/

238 https://www.forbes.com/pictures/efld45gghg/arrive-early/

239 https://www.hatchit.io/the-new-rules-of-job-hunting-during-covid19

240 https://enterprisersproject.com/article/2019/11/online-meeting-tips-6-best-practices

241 https://www.bcjobs.ca/blog/good-handshake-key-to-interview-success/

242 https://www.glassdoor.com/apps.htm

243 https://www.glassdoor.com/blog/job-search-tracker/

244 https://www.google.com/alerts

245 https://joinhandshake.com/students/how-it-works/

246 https://www.hellosign.com/

247 https://www.jibberjobber.com/login.php

248 https://itunes.apple.com/us/app/jobaware-job-search-just-got/id453682011?mt=8

249 https://play.google.com/store/apps/details?id=com.indeed.android.jobsearch&hl=en

250 https://blog.linkedin.com/2014/06/19/new-job-search-mobile-app

251 https://itunes.apple.com/us/app/linkedin-job-search/id886051313

252 https://play.google.com/store/apps/details?id=com.linkedin.android&hl=en_US

253 https://www.monster.com/

254 https://www.resumecoach.com/resume-templates/entry-level/

255 https://www.resumenerd.com/

256 https://www.resume-now.com/

257 https://www.snagajob.com/

258 https://itunes.apple.com/us/app/job-search-snagajob/id333188676?mt=8

259 https://play.google.com/store/apps/details?id=com.snagajob.jobseeker

260 https://zety.com/blog/teen-resume-example

261 https://www.ziprecruiter.com/

262 https://itunes.apple.com/us/app/ziprecruiter-job-search-free/id541933937?mt=8

263 https://play.google.com/store/apps/details?id=com.ziprecruiter.android.release&hl=en

264 https://99firms.com/blog/generation-z-statistics/#gref

265 https://visualcapitalist.com/meet-generation-z-the-newest-member-to-the-workforce

266 https://gladeo.org/

267 https://youtu.be/52ODbZN8naw

268 https://sso.teachable.com/secure/213035/users/sign_up?reset_purchase_session=1

269 https://vimeo.com/190206056

270 https://www.businessinsider.com/depression-increasing-among-millennials-gen-z-healthcare-burnout-2019-6

271 http://www.jeantwenge.com/

272 https://www.amazon.com/iGen-Super-Connected-Rebellious-Happy-Adulthood/dp/1501151983

273 https://thefutureorganization.com/future-gen-z-jlls-chro/

274 https://danschawbel.com/research/

275 https://www.theihanganeproject.com/

276 https://www.skees.org/story/announcing-hope-initiative-honor-jonah-hinman-promoting-wellbeing-hope-among-marginalized-people/

277 https://www.researchgate.net/profile/Kaye_Herth

278 https://www.skees.org/story/announcing-hope-initiative-honor-jonah-hinman-promoting-wellbeing-hope-among-marginalized-people/

279 https://www.newyorker.com/news/news-desk/how-the-survivors-of-parkland-began-the-never-again-movement

280 https://www.nytimes.com/2017/01/31/magazine/the-youth-group-that-launched-a-movement-at-standing-rock.html

281 https://www.linkedin.com/in/mayachawla/

282 https://zerocater.com/blog/2018/06/04/workforce-newest-members-generation-z/

283 https://www.myjobstories.org/

284 http://www.skees.org/

About the Authors

Sanam Yusuf, a proud member of Gen Z, is in her second year at Occidental College in Los Angeles, focusing on religious studies and diplomacy/world affairs. She had a transformational experience with Seeds of Peace International Camp, where  she was trained in dialogue and conflict resolution. She also spent five years as a delegate with Model United Nations (MUN). Through these experiences, she's been able to truly see the power of narratives and storytelling ... which is why she's so excited to be coauthoring this book!

Suzanne Skees, from the Boomer generation, is the author of the MY JOB[283] social-mission book series. She works in international development with the Skees Family Foundation[284], which supports innovative job-creation programs to end poverty. Skees studied English  literature at Boston College and world religions at Harvard Divinity School. She travels from schools to slums, prisons to farms, serving as a storyteller for nonprofit workers, social entrepreneurs, and their courageous clients who toil every day to create equality and end poverty.

Made in the USA
Middletown, DE
11 August 2021